B·O·N·S·A·I

B·O·N·S·A·i

IN COOPERATION WITH THE
BROOKLYN BOTANIC GARDEN

Susan M. Bachenheimer Resnick
Photographs by Kenro Izu
Foreword by Judith D. Zuk

LITTLE, BROWN AND COMPANY
BOSTON · TORONTO · LONDON

First American Edition

Conceived and produced by Swallow Books.

Library of Congress Catalog Card Number 91-58929

Library of Congress Cataloging-in-Publication
information is available

10 9 8 7 6 5 4 3 2 1

Published simultaneously in Canada by Little, Brown &
Company (Canada) Limited

Printed in Singapore

Unless otherwise indicated, all photographs were taken by
Kenro Izu at the Brooklyn Botanic Garden in New York.
The publisher wishes to thank the Brooklyn Botanic Garden
for allowing them to photograph the bonsai collection there.

Photographs: page 1, *Chaenomeles* x *superba*, Quince flower;
page 2, *left to right: Saikei* (details, page 105); *Juniperus
chinensis*, Sargent juniper (details, page 95); *Acer
buergerianum*, Trident maple (details, page 19); page 6
Tokyo garden.

Contents

Foreword

When the Brooklyn Botanic Garden received its first collection of 32 bonsai from Ernest F. Coe in 1925, the art of training dwarfed potted trees was scarcely known outside Japan. Over the last 65 years, as the Garden's collection has grown in number and complexity, so has western interest in this ancient form of horticulture.

BBG has played a significant role in fostering American interest in bonsai, through teaching courses, publishing handbooks and producing films and videos on the subject. Today, as our famous collection numbers more than 700 hardy and indoor specimens, we can easily say that bonsai is an internationally known and loved technique.

This surging increase in popularity has produced an equivalent need for solid information for the beginner and more advanced gardener. At BBG this has been evident to us, for our three bonsai handbooks remain our most popular titles. With the publication of Susan Resnick's book, we now have another valuable reference for bonsai enthusiasts. For the novice, this book provides straightforward information to start growing bonsai. The more experienced students will find inspiration in the beautiful illustrations and lively text. And both novice and expert will find the glossary invaluable for creating and maintaining successful bonsai.

This book will add to people's appreciation of the fine art of bonsai. We hope that it will give more people the courage to take up this beautiful, and enormously satisfying horticultural art.

Judith D. Zuk

Chapter 1
The History, Art and Philosophy of Bonsai

Bonsai. The word elicits varying reactions: admiration, curiosity, indifference. Enthusiasts practice the art for years, sometimes traveling halfway round the world to study with one of the handful of acknowledged bonsai masters. For these dedicated enthusiasts, bonsai can, and often does, quickly become a way of life. They are the people who stand before a display of well-grown examples and shed tears. Others turn away, unimpressed by the small trees in their even smaller containers, convinced that the trees are sick, or have been tortured. In fact, the reverse is true.

No matter what an individual's reaction to a single bonsai may be, bonsai cannot be easily dismissed. In China, where it probably originated, and in Japan, where the styles which are emulated around the world evolved, its associations with art and history, philosophy and religion are a dominant part of its mystique. Today, they are becoming better known in the West too.

This chapter sets out the history of bonsai and explains a little of the philosophy behind it, and how it came to be such a potent cultural symbol for so many people. An understanding of some of these factors, many of which are alien to Western thinking, will help to enhance your appreciation of this art form.

Pinus mugo *Swiss mountain pine*
A beautiful semicascade, this bonsai is about seventy years old, and has been part of the Brooklyn Botanic Garden Collection since 1972. These pines are hardy, able to withstand the harsh conditions of their native mountains. The white container with blue feet and a pine and crane design – both symbols of longevity – perfectly complements the bonsai. (Chest courtesy of Naga Antiques, New York.)

What is bonsai?

To the Japanese, there is a definite link between bonsai, nature, Man, and God. This partly arises from Zen Buddhist philosophy, which holds that spirituality can only be expressed through minimal aesthetic means, but it also goes deeper than this.

For the newcomer, probably the best way to understand the philosophy behind it is to start with the word itself. Bonsai (pronounced, contrary to popular belief, "bone-sigh"), literally translated, means "planted in a tray" or "potted dwarfed tree", depending on the translator. But it is important to remember, in addition, that bonsai is a living art. It compares with art forms that use paint and canvas, or marble and chisel, because bonsai too creates a composition and evokes emotional response by the sheer beauty of the material used and its container, and the effect of its stance and configuration on the viewer.

No one can say exactly when this art was first recognized and named, since bonsai developed without the benefit of specific written or visual documentation. It seems, however, that bonsai (known there as "*pen-jing*" or "*pun-sai*") were first cultivated in China. Only conjecture and educated guesses can paint the circumstances under which they developed to become such a powerful symbol to so many people in the civilized world.

The "plant in a tray" and the "potted dwarfed tree" have a long history. Evidence of them can be found, after careful scrutiny, in both pictorial pieces and in verbal or written records from centuries ago, some predating the birth of Christ. There is, for example, a Chinese legend dating from the Han dynasty (206 BC–AD 220) that ascribes the power to miniaturize landscapes, including trees, to one Fei Jiang Feng. Written records date from the third and fourth centuries, and it is clear that by the time of the T'ang dynasty (AD 618–906) bamboos, pines, and other plants were being grown in containers.

Interestingly, too, container plantings have been written about and artistically represented, in one form or another, in almost every sophisticated culture, both ancient and modern. The close relationship between nature, horticulture and human culture, as well as the respect for and exploration of that relationship, appears to have been an intrinsic part of many cultures from many parts of the world; these include the ancient Egyptians, Greeks and Romans, Persians and Hindus, among others.

It is not difficult to understand that, as people lived with plants every day, they would learn a great deal about them, including the fact that they could be packed up and taken along with migrating families, carried over long distances and difficult terrain, and re-established in the household when its members were newly settled. This process could

Sand garden in To-ji, Kyoto. Sand – and stone – gardens are common in Japan, and reflect the Zen Buddhist philosophy of austerity. In such gardens, two stones, juxtaposed in a certain way, can stand for the whole universe. This garden is modern, and depicts a well-known Japanese journey to China – the reverse of the journey that bonsai made. Different areas of the garden represent China and Japan, and rocks are used to represent a dragon, a turtle, and a knife.

Tomb of Nakht, Thebes, Egypt. This tomb painting from the 18th dynasty (c. 1500 BC) reflects the agrarian way of life of the period, and of the influence of crops – and therefore other plantings – on people's daily lives. Both functional and ornamental, plants provided medicine and fruit, as well as beauty. The Egyptians believed that painting scenes from life on the walls of their tombs gave the dead something familiar to relate to in the afterlife.

only have been successful if containers of a manageable size were used. Also, close proximity with those plantings would make it easier for their owners to know when they would flower, fruit, and so on. Such constant observation would give growers sufficient knowledge to enable them to manipulate factors such as the time of bloom and even the copiousness of fruit production. Thus for the New Year a Chinese family, for example, could look forward to the presence of the flowering apricot. As one of the earliest spring-flowering trees to produce blossoms (in many bonsai nurseries in Tokyo today, apricots are in full bloom at the end of February), the apricot became a powerful and important symbol of the end of winter and a harbinger of the good springtime to come.

There was a strong horticultural tradition in ancient Egypt. In their pottery, carvings, and drawings – some of which have been found in the temples near Thebes which were built over 4000 years ago – the Egyptians depicted trees in containers, and trees growing in rock crevices. It appears from contemporary works of art that trees were brought great distances to enhance the formal garden of Queen Hatshepsut. Pharaoh Rameses III was reputed to have encouraged the development of gardens within his temples, and the use of potted plants of all kinds, including olives, lotuses, rushes, lilies, date palms, and grasses, to decorate them.

Hindus practiced the science of dwarfing trees in order to insure that they had to hand the substances used in the healing science of Ayurvedic medicine, known throughout India and still practiced today.

Container planting was adopted in almost every sophisticated early culture, then tailored to suit the multiplicity of climates and ways of life in different countries. Consequently, growers' understanding of the nuances of raising and keeping plants became more and more refined, as they became more aware of the detailed relationship between sun and soil, water and nutrients, and the ultimate well-being of their potted plants. Garden planning and design grew in importance, and plants in containers became an integral feature of both formal and informal gardens.

China, Japan, and the West

In the West, probably the major development from this container tradition was topiary. Westerners were particularly enamored of the practice of pruning plants into familiar geometric shapes and animal forms. Geometric and animal shapes created from live plants were known in the reign of the Emperor Augustus at the time of the birth of Christ.

Over the years, gardeners in England, France, Italy, and the United States advanced topiary skills by creating whole theme gardens around a collection of diverse subjects, including everything from elephants and giraffes, dragons and squirrels, to chessmen and geometric spirals.

While, however, both the bonsai and topiary traditions of pruning and shaping attempt to create realistic shapes artificially, artistically the two are in complete opposition.

The practice of topiary demands the development and pruning of a mass of foliage into a recognizable form that frequently exhibits great humor, along with style and, often, improbability.

The Japanese technique of bonsai differs. Its history embraces many cultural symbols with serious overtones. For the Japanese, bonsai represents a fusion of strong

ancient beliefs and practices, and a manifestation of the Eastern philosophy of harmony between man and nature. There is irrefutable evidence that, for centuries, the Japanese included horticultural symbolism in their homes and in their religious ceremonies, some in the form of especially revered plants.

It is possible that bonsai had crossed the waters from China to Japan by AD 1195, since there appears to be a reference to it in a Japanese scroll attributed to that period. It is probable that Buddhist monks introduced bonsai to Japan, since it fits naturally their philosophy of love and reverence for nature and age.

Kan Yashiroda, a bonsai master and author, in his documentation of the history of bonsai, however, believes that a picture scroll by Takakane Takashina, called *Kasugagongen-genki* and painted in 1309 during the Kamakura period (1180–1333), is the earliest and most reliable record of the existence of bonsai. From the same period, he cites a scroll describing the life of Honen and showing a variety of small trees in containers. Some experts believe these containers to be ceramic and almost certainly made specifically for housing these small trees.

Yashiroda also makes reference to the *Tsurezure-gusa*, a piece written in that period by Kenko Yoshida, who says: "To appreciate and find pleasure in curiously curved potted trees is to love deformity." Whether that is a positive or negative comment, these and other clues have led many experts to believe that growing dwarfed and twisted trees in

containers was an accepted practice among the Japanese upper class of the Kamakura period. If that is true, and bonsai was a highly refined art form by the fourteenth century, then it is very likely that it had been practiced for many years before that time.

More than one bonsai researcher has mentioned the Noh play *Hachi-no-ki*, or *Tree in the Container*, written by Seami during the Muromachi period (1363–1444). In it, a poor man, once prosperous, gives refuge to a beggar during a snowstorm. The night is bitter and the poor man has no wood with which to heat his hut. He remembers that outside remain the last three bonsai from a once great collection and, in an act of sacrifice, he offers to burn them to keep the beggar warm. The beggar, actually a retired Regent of the Kamakura shogunate, refuses his more than generous offer. Yet the poor man, knowing he will be forever warmed by the memories of caring for his bonsai, grooming them and loving their beauty, sets fire to them to keep his uninvited guest warm.

Bonsai became an important part of upper-class Japanese life, with the little trees brought inside for specific occasions, to reside temporarily upon specially designed shelves. No longer were they permanently relegated only to outdoor display. However, the practices of pruning and training as we know them today did not develop until later.

By the seventeenth century, Japanese gardening and garden design were at their zenith. In fact, all the arts were strongly encouraged and appreciated by a government at

LEFT: *Levens Hall, Cumbria, England, 1879. Topiary has been called the Western response to bonsai, since both rely on trying to create natural shapes using plants. The resemblance ends there, however. The modern topiary tradition stems from formal gardens of the seventeenth century, like the one pictured here. Animals, birds, anchors, and teddy bears have all been used in these gardens, as have geometric shapes such as spheres and cones. Topiary is also often used in creating screens and mazes.*

RIGHT: *Lovers under a Mosquito Net. This Japanese print by Koyusai (1721–89) shows an informal upright bonsai just outside the screened area. The Edo period was characterized by the rise of a merchant class, and state control over the lives of all citizens. One result of this strict control, coupled with a total ban on contact with foreign cultures, was the preservation of traditional esthetics and values. The role of bonsai as an important cultural artifact developed during this period of isolation.*

peace with itself and the world. In the early eighteenth century, the art of bonsai was overseen by Ibei Ito, whose nursery features in a contemporary painting owned by Kan Yashiroda. The bonsai depicted in the painting, according to Yashiroda, are grown in a variety of styles and formed from a variety of plants, although the containers in which they are growing seem to have been slightly deeper than those used today.

Probably the major factor in maintaining the art of bonsai was the removal of all but the most important portions of the plant. You will read more about this in the later chapters. This ''reduction to the essentials'' was also reflected in many different art forms of the period.

Which came first, the approach to artwork or bonsai, is indeterminable. What matters is that this same minimalism is found in the line drawings that dominated Japanese screens, and that the most popular form of poetry of the period was the sparingly worded, four-lined and seventeen-syllabled piece named *Haiku*. Design in many areas was reduced to its most salient features. So it was with bonsai.

As time passed, bonsai began to take on varied styles, some realistic, some naturalistic, but all more closely embodying the spirit of the plants used. In the 1850s, after more than 250 years of isolationism, Japan opened her boundaries to trade with the rest of the world, and travelers started to bring back from Japan stories of the miniature trees in small containers, in which a very complex and closely held tradition of care was ''concealed''. The art of

bonsai assumed a cloak of mystery which has surrounded it to this day.

In China, meanwhile, the art was also evolving, again very largely in isolation from the rest of the world. After the opium wars of 1839–42, the Royal Horticultural Society in London sponsored a trip to China by plant-hunter Robert Fortune, ostensibly to look at tea-growing. He wrote of the methods of Chinese bonsaiists in 1853, that they selected already stunted plants or small seeds for training, and then twisted the stems in order to check the flow of sap (and thereby limit the plant's growth). The plants were confined to narrow, shallow pots containing a small amount of soil and watered only sufficiently to keep them alive. His account continued: ''Whilst the branches were forming, they were tied down and twisted in various ways, the points of the leaders and strong growing ones were generally nipped out, and every means was taken to discourage the production of young shoots which were possessed of any degree of vigour.''

In Japan at this time bonsaiists were gradually introducing other culturally important elements into their small compositions; these included rocks, small buildings, bridges, and people. They may have reproduced actual landscapes in miniature to remind them of pleasant times or important events. Certainly, during Japan's isolation from the rest of the world (and, to a certain extent, after it had ended) tourism and travel within Japan became the most popular leisure pursuits for the masses, and the majority of the population bought illustrations and prints of the country's major tourist attractions.

By the end of the nineteenth century, interest abroad in all things Japanese was at its height, fuelled by the Japanese presence at the international exhibitions in London (1862), Vienna (1873), and Paris (1867 and 1900), and an animated trade in Eastern plants had begun. With the trade came visitors, many of whom saw for the first time and coveted the small trees in containers. Professional collectors, sponsored by arboreta and private businesses, also began a

LEFT: *Kyuzo Murata's garden in Omiya, outside Tokyo, the bonsai capital of Japan, is not only dedicated to bonsai. There are areas in which he grows full-size plants and flowers, and also grasses and mosses to add to his bonsai containers.*

RIGHT: *Stone lantern ornament from Mr Ueda's garden in Ibaraki, near Osaka. We tend to think of formal ornaments as typically Western, but they are also used in Japanese gardens, to lighten the austerity, or to provide a focal point.*

systematic search for naturally dwarfed material that bore the unmistakable marks of nature's weathering effects, and the struggle to survive.

It was then that these factors gave rise to an industry, for it was then that the reduction in numbers of available natural dwarfs and the growing demand for bonsai inspired the Japanese to establish nurseries solely for the purpose of growing, training, and then exporting trees. They also realized that plants that had naturally smaller and neater foliage and growth habits were a logical choice with which to work, so new trees started to become popular for bonsai, and the growers introduced them to bonsai culture.

With the increased and profitable demand, technical skills such as raising bonsai from seed and cuttings, and the styling and grafting of unusual, difficult or tender material onto hardy root stock, were further developed. The techniques have been so perfected that today any bonsai that bears the slightest evidence of wiring or pruning is considered inferior.

Thus, the Japanese began purposefully to prune and cultivate their potted trees in shapes which approximated those seen for centuries in brush paintings and scrolls, and in styles appreciated by enthusiasts.

Bonsai today

The art of bonsai has evolved to reflect changing tastes and times, as well as the great variety of countries, cultures, and conditions in which it is practiced.

It is common in Japan to stroll through a residential or business area and see bonsai in the window of the laundry or drugstore, as well as in ordinary homes. They grow on balconies, on terraces, on window ledges. The Daimaru department store above Tokyo Station has given over its roof space to bonsai, and a bonsai exhibition is held annually in the store. They silently reside against the backdrop of the side of a house or take in the sun ensconced in a tiny courtyard. White pines are seen at corporate meetings, placed prominently on the speaker's dais. The New Year is not complete unless the *tokonoma* – the special niche in every Japanese home used for the display of ornaments and prized possessions – is filled with a blossoming apricot or plum tree. And collections of bonsai are passed from father to son, treasured examples of shared experience and the continuation of the family.

In Japan, bonsai is no longer confined to the upper class, but a joy shared by factory worker and company president

Traditional-style tokonoma *at the Yonan-so Hotel, Utsunomiya. There are many other traditional Japanese features in this* tokonoma. *The moveable screens, or* shoji, *the modular* tatami *mat, and the calligraphy on the scroll are all aspects of the Japanese minimalism that characterizes bonsai – the stripping away of all but the essentials, so that the essence of an object is revealed.*

Street scene in modern Tokyo. The Japanese can create a garden or raise and care for bonsai in a strip of space a yard wide. A natural retreat from the overcrowded, noisy city, the Japanese garden provides a haven of tranquillity.

alike. Each brings appreciation, concern, care, and pride to his bonsai (interestingly, and in contrast to the Western experience, bonsai in Japan, *is* predominantly a male preserve), whether it is a bonsai-in-training or a recognized national treasure. Those who have large private collections and incomes to match hire professionals to do the routine maintenance or to make crucial decisions about possible style changes.

Understandably, the Japanese prefer to concentrate on using native plants, which offer a vast array of choice candidates for bonsai culture. Indeed, typically Japanese varieties are also admired and coveted throughout the rest of the world, even in those countries without a strong oriental tradition. Excursions into exotic material from alien climates therefore is minimal in Japan and going to outside sources for appropriate plants is considered largely unnecessary – native plant life is sufficiently all-encompassing in character.

The one dark cloud on the horizon, however, is Japan's rapidly diminishing countryside. The Japanese suffer more than most other industrialized countries from urban sprawl and the meeting of city boundary with city boundary, with little of the original landscape in between. Perhaps this is why bonsai is so important in Japanese culture, and why it is becoming more popular in the West.

Nonetheless, in the urban sprawl outside Tokyo lies the town of Omiya. It is still charming, its streets dotted with small, beautifully designed gardens and courtyards. In many, clusters of bonsai are gathered near the front doors so both passersby and residents can enjoy their message. It could be that, to the octogenarian dozing peacefully in his family's courtyard, seeing the bonsai forest can take him back through the years to a similar forest where, as a young boy, he spent time in a place that has now become a victim of the advance of the city. There is a monument in Omiya to the founder of the town's first bonsai nursery – Mr Shimizu. A bonsai master who had a nursery in Tokyo, he chose to move from the unfavorable conditions of the city after the 1923 earthquake and fire. He settled on Omiya as somewhere more suitable to cultivate his plants and, in 1925, founded a nursery there. In this town, various specimens that today make up some of the world's major collections began their lives. Here, rather than being fenced or placed on a pedestal or pronounced "out of bounds", the plants are completely accessible. They almost reach out and draw viewers of all ages into a miniature world. Neighborhood children take their toy horses and deer to graze in the velvety moss beneath hundred-year-old trees. To a small child, a grove of miniature trees can become a forest of magnificent old ones, even if that fantasy lasts only a few hours.

So, while bonsai is indeed an ancient art, bonsai as we know it today has truly flowered over the past 150 years, with its cultivation and appreciation spreading to every corner of an ever-shrinking world.

Chapter 2
A Gallery of Bonsai

There is no doubt that one of the best ways to understand good bonsai and appreciate the particular qualities that make them so special, is to visit as many collections and exhibitions as you can to see some of the supreme examples of the bonsaiist's art. Where you live, obviously, has some bearing on the ease with which you might be able to do this, and this chapter gives the location of some of the major collections in the world that are open to the public.

It is important to realize, however, that no two bonsai are the same. As you will see from the photographs throughout this book, trees belonging to the same species, of a similar age, and grown under comparable conditions differ widely – as indeed they do in nature. What looking at the best examples of bonsai will give you is an insight into why they are so beautiful, in other words the natural characteristics that the bonsaiist has managed to reproduce so faithfully. From this it follows that looking at trees in general, particularly in the countryside or in woodland where Man's intervention is reduced, will help you to train your eye to recognize some of these characteristics. The Japanese believe that the trunk is the most important part of the tree in bonsai, followed by the branches, then the leaves. Look at all these on the trees around you, and consider the bonsai in the photographs that follow in the light of your knowledge. Your aim as a bonsaiist will be to maintain or to reproduce the natural look of those mature trees.

Acer buergerianum *Trident maple*
This informal upright bonsai was a gift from the city of Tokyo to the city of New York, and became part of the Brooklyn Botanic Garden Collection in 1961. Acquired from Kyuka-en, Kyuzo Murata's nursery in Omiya, this tree is estimated to be 114 years old and sits in an oval, light-blue glazed container. The entire bonsai, including container, measures 37 × 30 inches and is 37 inches high.

Bonsai on show

Bonsai exhibitions cannot be said to be frequent anywhere except Japan, although they are occasionally held in the West, and there has been a bonsai stand at the famous Chelsea Flower Show in London since 1960. Most are mounted under the auspices of one of the major collections. However, there are bonsai clubs and societies in many regions of the United States and Canada, and you should contact your local state organization for information about meetings and exhibitions.

In the East, such exhibitions are rare in China, although they are fairly frequent in Hong Kong. Most exhibitions of bonsai open to the public are, unsurprisingly, held in Japan. The National Diet Bonsai exhibition in November is followed in early December by the Nippon Bonsai Taikan exhibition. The Nippon Bonsai Sakufu exhibition is held in January in the Daimaru department store (see p. 16). The Kokofu exhibition, which is held in February, was established at the Tokyo Metropolitan Art Museum in 1934, and this is followed in April/May by the Osaka exhibition (held on the site of Expo 70), which is organized by the Nippon Bonsai Association. In August, the Mitsukoshi department store opens its doors to the country's many bonsai enthusiasts.

Catalogs from these exhibitions offer an indication to outsiders of the quality of trees on display. The exposure given to any tree featured in any of them is likely to result in an increase in its value.

The major collections

The best bonsai collections in the world – both public and private – are in Japan, and the principal nurseries are in Omiya (see p. 17). Two of the premier figures in the Japanese bonsai world are Kyuzo Murata, owner of the Kyuka-en Collection, and Saburo Kato, who owns the Mansei-en Collection, both of which are situated in Omiya and both of which are open to the public. Both masters are consultants to the Emperor of Japan's Collection, probably the finest in the world, and certainly the finest collection of bonsai in the "grand style", and also to the Princess Chichibu Collection. Saburo Kato is one of three brothers, all of whom are bonsai masters, and the son of one of the founders of Omiya. The other major collections in Japan are the Oguchi Collection in Okaya City, the Sudo Collection, near Utsunomiya, and the Ueda Collection, near Osaka.

Roadside sign, Omiya, Japan. This wooden signpost directs visitors to the various permanent bonsai exhibitions, all of which are open to the public, and which form just a small sample of the bonsai nurseries situated in Omiya. From the top: Fujo-en, Mansei-en (the collection owned by Saburo Kato), Kyuka-en (owned by Kyuzo Murata), Shoto-en and Seika-en. There are photographs of bonsai from the Mansei-en and Kyuka-en Collections throughout this book.

OPPOSITE *Pinus parviflora* Japanese white pine *Imported from Japan in 1961, this magnificent tree has no container but is planted directly onto an irregularly shaped rock slab. Overall, the bonsai measures 48 × 36 inches, including the slab, and is 32 inches high. It is estimated to be about sixty-nine years old, and accompanied the trident maple on p. 18 to New York.*

20

In the United States, the major collections open to the public are the National Bonsai and Penjing Museum at the National Arboretum in Washington DC (probably the best collection outside Japan, this includes fifty-three trees given by the people of Japan to the American people in 1976 to celebrate the Bicentenary); the Arnold Arboretum's Larz Anderson Bonsai Collection in Jamaica Plain, Massachusetts; the Pacific Rim Bonsai Collection in Seattle, Washington; and the Brooklyn Botanic Garden Collection in New York. In Canada, the Montreal Botanical Garden also has a fine bonsai collection open to the public.

Europe is less well served. There are no national collections in the United Kingdom, France or Germany, where the major examples of bonsai are owned by individual bonsai masters and enthusiasts. Among them, Paul Lesniewicz in Heidelberg, Germany, Rémy Samson in Paris, France, and Peter Chan in Surrey, England, have probably the finest collections.

This chapter illustrates some of the most important and most beautiful bonsai from the collection at the Brooklyn Botanic Garden in New York. This collection is typical for many reasons. Its bonsai trees arrived at the Garden in a variety of different ways: some came directly from Japan; others were donated by keen bonsaiists who had imported and raised them themselves; still others were created at the Garden by its skilled bonsai masters. The trees span a wide age range: the current oldest – the beautiful *Pinus parviflora* (Japanese white pine) pictured on p. 27 – is about 265 years old, although its oldest tree ever was a *Juniperus chinensis* 'Sargentii' (Sargent juniper), colloquially

21

known as "Fudo", which was 850 years old when it became part of the Brooklyn Collection in 1971. Unfortunately it died a slow death in the following year. It is still, however, on display, its graceful, curving trunk looking as artistic in death as it ever did in life.

The collection also includes trees of different sizes, from miniature or *mame* bonsai – those standing less than 7 inches high – to large examples – technically, up to 4 feet, and from many species, ranging from the "typical" Japanese subjects such as *Acer palmatum* (Japanese maple) to native American material (much of which is also suitable for northern Europe). It is probably atypical only in the fact that it contains a great number of indoor bonsai. Since the 1960s, as part of its commitment to research, the Brooklyn Botanic Garden has been at the forefront of work with indoor bonsai. Pioneering work by Frank Okamura, the gardener in charge of bonsai, and his successor, Kazuo Fujii, has helped to make the collection of indoor trees, which now number more than 200, one of the best in the world. A major exhibition mounted in 1976 showed just how far research on these trees had progressed.

Bonsai at the BBG

Although the Brooklyn Botanic Garden was inaugurated in 1909, and a Japanese Hill and Pond Garden – designed by landscape artist Takeo Shiota – was completed in 1914, the history of its bonsai only really began in 1925, when Ernest Coe, a nurseryman from Connecticut, gave the Garden 32 bonsai which he had imported from Japan. He was retiring to Florida and realized that his outdoor trees would not survive long in the warm climate. Fifteen years before, when the cost of importing a bonsai from Japan was still being quoted in gold, the value of these trees might have drawn more attention but unfortunately it did not, and so many of the trees that comprised this donation perished.

The Second World War was probably the catalyst in reviving interest in bonsai at the Garden – as indeed it was in many other countries. The appointment of George Avery as Director in 1944, and the arrival of Frank Okamura to take care of the Japanese Garden and the bonsai, both of whom were interested in the small trees, also helped in this. According to the charter by which it was founded, the BBG had been conceived:

"... for the collection and culture of plants, flowers, shrubs, and trees, the advancement of botanical science and knowledge, and the prosecution of original

researches therein and in kindred subjects; for affording instruction in the same . . . and for the entertainment, recreation and instruction of the people . . ." (New York State Charter, 1897).

It was the educational aspects of these goals that became particularly important in the context of the bonsai at the Garden. American GIs, returning from Japan at the end of

TRIDENT MAPLE
ACER BUERGERANUM
C. 91 YEARS OLD IN 1988
GIFT OF THE CITY OF TOKYO

The Garden's bonsai were moved to the C.V. Starr Bonsai Museum of the new Steinhardt Conservatory in 1988. They are arranged in two groups: the outdoor and indoor bonsai. The outdoor specimens (essentially temperate deciduous or evergreen trees, and conifers) require winter temperatures during their dormant periods; these are displayed on pedestals and wooden benches. The indoor bonsai are tropical and warm temperate species, which need a controlled climate in order to survive. These are housed in a glass case.

the War, brought with them either finished bonsai, or a knowledge and experience of and exposure to bonsai, and wanted to know more about them and how to care for them. The first handbook on bonsai was published in 1953, under the guest editorship of Kan Yashiroda (see pp. 13–14), who probably did more than any other individual to bring an understanding of the horticulture of Japan to the West.

Since then, two further handbooks and an instructional video have been produced, and numerous demonstrations, seminars, exhibits, and courses on bonsai – attended by visitors from all over the world – have been held.

The photographs that follow are the result of the years of painstaking work, research, care, and understanding, both in Japan and at the Garden, on the bonsai in its Collection.

LEFT: Acer buergerianum
Trident maple
An informal upright mame, or
miniature, bonsai, this trident
maple was propagated by Frank
Okamura from a cutting taken
from the forest shown on p. 34,
in 1960. After eight years"
initial training, it was planted
in the oval, brown unglazed
container in 1968. Including its
container, this bonsai measures
just 7 × 6 inches, and is 8½
inches high.
  (Chest courtesy of Naga
Antiques, New York.)

LEFT AND BELOW: Carpinus
japonica *Japanese hornbeam*
Without its deeply grooved
leaves, the stunning architecture
of the trunk and the fine
ramification of the branches,
typical of Japanese hornbeams
and normally hidden by the mass
of foliage, can be clearly seen.
An informal upright imported
from Kyuzo Murata's nursery
in 1961, this bonsai is estimated
to be seventy-six years old and is
planted in a rectangular
stippled light and dark blue
container.

Sequoia sempervirens *Redwood*
A formal upright created by
Frank Okamura in the 1960s,
this redwood has been in the
same oval glazed green and tan
moiré container for more than
twenty-five years. Estimated to be
thirty-nine years old, it measures
24 × 20 inches and is 17½ inches
high overall.

RIGHT: Pinus parviflora
Japanese white pine
An informal upright bonsai
estimated to be about 265 years
old (which makes it the oldest
currently in the Brooklyn
Botanic Garden Collection), this
Japanese white pine was
originally collected in the wild,
from the mountains of Shikoku

Island in Japan. It was
imported into the United States
in 1964 from Kyuka-en.
Originally housed in a brown
unglazed earthenware container,
it now grows in a round blue and
brown mottled glazed container
that is 7 inches high. Overall,
this bonsai measures 30 × 28
inches and is 38 inches high.

LEFT AND ABOVE: **Acer**
palmatum *Japanese maple*
One of the first bonsai in the
Brooklyn Botanic Garden's
Collection, this beautiful
Japanese maple was donated by
Ernest Coe (see p. 22) in 1925.
Positioned in a round brown
earthtone unglazed container
with a scalloped rim, it is
estimated to be ninety-six years
old and overall measures 36×28
inches, by 33 inches high. The
container has a diameter of
$16\frac{1}{2}$ inches and is $5\frac{1}{2}$ inches
high.

LEFT: Juniperus horizontalis
Creeping juniper
This informal upright bonsai
was created at the Brooklyn
Botanic Garden by Frank
Okamura in the early 1970s, as
part of a demonstration to
students. The oval unglazed
brown container is 8 × 4½ inches,
by 1¼ inches high. The bonsai
measures 8 × 6 inches, and is 8
inches high.

Ilex serrata
Japanese winterberry
This forest of five trees is
believed to be fifty-one years old,
although it was only imported
from Kyuka-en to the United
States in 1964. It measures
24 × 18 inches and stands 18
inches high overall. The two-tone
blue moiré effect glazed oval
container is 3 inches high, and
measures 16 × 9 inches.

LEFT: Rhododendron obtusum 'Amoenum' Kirishima or Hiryu azalea
Estimated to be seventy-nine years old, this slanting style bonsai was a gift to the Garden Collection in 1972. In spring, it is a mass of shocking pink flowers. The round brown unglazed container is 14 inches in diameter and 5¾ inches high. It was one of the largest bonsai displayed in an exhibition of bonsai at the Rockefeller Center in New York City in 1981, its overall dimensions being 27 × 24 inches. It stands 35 inches high.

Wisteria floribunda
Japanese wisteria
This wisteria was transplanted from the Japanese Garden at the Brooklyn Botanic Garden by Frank Okamura in 1947. He root- and top-pruned it for fourteen years until, in 1961, he judged it to be ready for planting in this round blue glazed container 10 inches in diameter and 7 inches high. An informal upright, this bonsai measures 24 × 13 inches and is 29 inches high overall. Confining wisterias to small pots such as the one above ensures good flower production.

ABOVE: Acer buergerianum
Trident maple
A seventy-three-year-old forest of seven trees imported in 1957 from the Tokyo nursery of Yuji Yoshimura. (Mr Yoshimura wrote one of the earliest books on bonsai published in English and owns a collection in New York State, open to the public by appointment only). The trees are planted in the root-over-rock style in a blue-green antique Chinese container.

OPPOSITE: Celtis sinensis
Chinese or Japanese hackberry
An eighty-year-old formal upright, this bonsai is planted in an oval brown earthtone unglazed container measuring $18 \times 13\frac{1}{2}$ inches and $1\frac{3}{4}$ inches high. It was imported from Kyuka-en in 1961, and overall measures 16×16 inches, by 29 inches high.

ABOVE: Pinus parviflora
Japanese white pine
This Japanese white pine bonsai
was created by Frank Okamura.
It is an informal upright style
where the high top was grafted to
the trunk in the early 1960s. It
was kept in a nursery container
until 1982 when Kazuo Fujii
placed it in its rectangular
brown earthtone unglazed
container. Its training was
continued after this, and today it
measures 15 × 10 inches, by 17
inches high.

RIGHT: Pinus parviflora
Japanese white pine
By contrast, this Japanese white
pine (also called five-needle
pine) was collected in the wild —
as opposed to being raised from
seed or a cutting, or by grafting —
and was imported from Omiya
in 1964. A windswept style rock
planting, it measures 32 × 32
inches and is 27 inches high
overall. It occupies an unglazed
brown earthtone container and is
estimated to be ninety-four
years old.

ABOVE: Chaenomeles japonica
Japanese flowering quince
This bonsai first produced its
pale yellow flowers in 1977,
when it was estimated to be
sixty-three years old. Imported
in 1964 from Japan, it is a
multistem shrub-style planting
and occupies a round brown
earthtone container with a
scalloped rim. This bonsai
measures 24 × 18 inches, and is
24 inches high.

Serissa foetida *"Variegata"*
Variegated snow rose
A thirty-year-old bonsai, this
was created by Frank Okamura
as a class demonstration in the
1960s. It is a multitrunk shrub-
style planting, with small white
flowers and variegated leaves. It
grows in a rectangular brown
earthtone unglazed container.
This bonsai featured in the 1976
exhibition of indoor bonsai at the
Brooklyn Botanic Garden.

Chapter 3
Choosing and Buying Bonsai

Buying a finished bonsai, and learning how to keep it in good condition through such routine tasks as feeding and watering, is an ideal introduction to the art of bonsai. Although creating your own bonsai may be the ultimate goal, this approach has several advantages: you will become familiar with all the techniques of care and maintainance; you will learn which plants suit your lifestyle and the conditions that you can offer them; and you will not be discouraged by a possible failure in these early stages. It is logical to postpone attempts at creating bonsai until you know that you can deal confidently with any problems you might encounter.

A few years ago, when the art of bonsai was still in its infancy in the West, this chapter probably would not have been necessary. At that time, most people who purchased bonsai were already bonsai enthusiasts, with some knowledge of and exposure to quality trees. Today, this picture has changed considerably. Bonsai are being produced and sold in greater numbers than ever before. Quality, however, is often variable and this, combined with the fact that many buyers are inexperienced, has made the purchase of bonsai more hazardous.

In cities like London, New York and Paris, it is not unusual to see bonsai in department stores, alongside gourmet chocolates and other luxury items. With so many enthusiasts buying finished bonsai, some guidance on what to look for is vital.

Lespedeza cyrtobotrya *Bush clover*
Bush clover, a shrub with beautiful purplish-rose flowers, is often grown to accompany other bonsai, as part of a forest or a saikei, for example. This bonsai bush clover from the Ueda Collection is grown in the clump style. The fine branches and small leaves and flowers make it particularly suitable for this treatment.

Choosing the right plant

If you are buying your first bonsai, the most important consideration is to choose a plant that is suited to your abilities and to the conditions of care that you can offer.

There is no point in buying the most expensive bonsai in the shop just because you can afford it. If you collect Chippendale furniture or modern paintings, buying the best may make sense. But bonsai is a living art form. The plants are not static, but constantly developing and changing. To maintain the form that the artist has achieved after years of work requires diligence and knowledge. Plants must be watered, fed, pruned, pinched, repotted, and wired at the proper time. Improper handling or neglect can very quickly make a mess of a masterpiece.

The best first bonsai are moderately priced. The kind you choose will depend, of course, on your growing conditions, but generally you will be most successful with species that have a vigorous, almost weed-like capacity for growth. Needled junipers, most tropical plants, elms, *Chamaecyparis*, crabapple, *Pyracantha* and most flowering trees are generally forgiving. If you make a pruning mistake, or forget to pinch foliage, these plants will sprout new growth that can eventually be trained to hide the error. They also require fairly frequent grooming, which helps beginners become familiar with their new bonsai through constant observation and handling. Pines and spruces, on the other hand, are slow growing and unforgiving. Growth occurs only at the tips of branches, so mistakes made on the lower portions of these trees are permanent. They are best avoided by beginners. (Not for indoors.)

You should consider, too, the conditions under which you will grow and keep the plants when choosing bonsai. If you live in an apartment, choose tropical or semi-tropical species that can grow indoors all year round (see pp. 120–41) and avoid temperate plants, such as pines, spruces, junipers, and Japanese maples. While these are classic subjects, each requires a period of cold, winter dormancy of between six weeks and three months. If you cannot overwinter temperate bonsai in a cold-frame or other suitable position outdoors, or in a garage or unheated sun porch, consider a tropical or semi-tropical bonsai instead. Also, match your choice of tree to the available light. If your only window faces north into a courtyard, you cannot expect a sun-worshipper like pomegranate to thrive.

Some beginners find it impossible to resist buying strictly outdoor trees such as pines precisely because they evoke nature so powerfully, and indeed success with such trees may even seem within reach for a year or two as needles and leaves grow larger and larger. Unfortunately, such growth is often also overly soft, uneven and sporadic. It is a fact that temperate bonsai eventually decline and die if they are kept warm in winter.

Determining age and quality

Once you have decided what kind of tree to buy, how do you tell which one is the better specimen? Is age important? Is a 25-year-old tree automatically more valuable than a 15-year-old? And why do some shops label a plant with both "age" and "age in training"? Is there a difference?

The question of age can be most confusing to newcomers. While it is true that a specimen that *appears* ancient is highly prized, its actual age is not that important. In fact, actual age is hard to determine unless the grower raised the plant from seed. Growth rates vary tremendously depending on the conditions under which the plant was cultivated, and such factors as the water, light, and fertilizer it received. It is also impossible to tell age by the thickness of the trunk or the size of the tree. One of the only accurate

ways to determine age – used in bonsai nurseries – is by using an increment borer: a hollow tube which is inserted into the trunk to remove a thin core of tree rings. Scientists can gauge the approximate age by counting the rings.

There are, however, many difficulties in determining age by trunk thickness. A dead *Cryptomeria* at an expert's bonsai nursery (even experts lose trees sometimes) had grown so slowly that its rings were hairline thin and closely packed. Although the number of rings (one for each year of growth) revealed that the tree was more than 500 years old, the stump, incredibly, was only 3 inches in diameter. Then there is the famous avenue of immense *Cryptomeria* at the temples at Nikko, in Japan. These trees are less than 400 years old, yet some of their trunks are more than 6 feet in diameter.

If actual age is difficult to determine, age in training is easy, since it is just a matter of keeping accurate records on each plant. Even without documentation, however, you can often spot well-grown bonsai that have been in cultivation for a long time. Trunks are usually well tapered and thick at the base, branches are highly articulated, and large limbs taper into a well-developed network of successively smaller branches, much as you would see on a mature tree outdoors.

It is difficult, of course, to generalize about what makes a good bonsai since there are so many styles of training, so many kinds of trees and so many moods that they evoke. A single, upright pine with jagged gray bark may remind you of an imposing, dignified forest patriarch. The attraction of a group of Japanese maples, on the other hand, might be the lyrical appeal of their spreading surface roots and shapely curves – you can almost hear birds chirping in their branches on a sunny morning.

Yet although the mood of each bonsai is different, the attraction of good bonsai is that they do evoke such powerful emotions through one or more strong design elements. Rugged bark, a thick and twisting trunk, and dense masses of foliage convey great power and dignity. Trunks with ancient-looking cavities, bleached dead wood, and contorted branches suggest great strength under adversity. A shapely, curving trunk and delicate tracery of branches are reminiscent of the beauty of spring-flowering trees growing in the shadows of forest giants.

Whatever the style, however, always make sure that the bonsai you choose is healthy. Look closely at all live branches: they should have leaves that have good color and are unblemished. Although some bonsai may have more

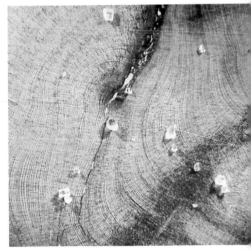

LEFT: Picea *sp. Spruce*
An excellent example of a mame *or miniature bonsai, this slanting style spruce was trained for several years before being placed in its rectangular green glazed container – measuring $2\frac{1}{2} \times 1\frac{3}{4}$ inches, by 1 inch high – in 1970. Spruces, like pines, must have a period of winter cold, so are not the best choice if you live in an apartment. They are also slow-growing which can be frustrating to a beginner. They are, however, favored trees for bonsai in the United States in particular, and are well suited to temperate conditions. Overall, this particular bonsai measures 6×5 inches, and is 5 inches high.*
(Chest courtesy of Naga Antiques, New York.)

Pine tree in the garden of Ginkaku-ji, Kyoto. Pines are undoubtedly the most popular bonsai subjects, suitable for training in a variety of styles. Pinus densiflora (Japanese red pine) is the most common

species in Japan, although both Pinus parviflora (Japanese white pine), with its purple-brown bark, and Pinus thunbergii (Japanese black pine) tend to be more common in bonsai.

Cross-section through the trunk of a shrubby tree found growing on a Canadian cliff. Thought to be 400 years old, the tree is only 2–3 feet tall. Each grain of sugar covers an average of fifteen years' growth.

artistic dead wood than live branches and appear to be barely clinging to life, this should only be an artistic illusion. Live parts of the tree should be vigorous. There should be no leaf spots, or yellow or brown leaves (although some deciduous trees, such as oaks and beeches, normally retain their dead, brown leaves throughout winter). Look for a well-groomed plant with no insects. Roots should not be growing out of the drainage holes at the bottom of the pot. Live branches should be unbroken and free from wiring scars.

Experts will sometimes purchase bonsai that are not in especially good condition because they see possibilities behind the neglect. With proper care and deft restyling in artistic hands, such specimens can be nursed back to health and metamorphose into spectacular trees. However, this is an area best left to experts. Novices are often eager to begin reshaping before a tree is in good enough health to take the added stress, so poor trees do tend to decline and die in inexperienced hands. It is far more encouraging to begin with good bonsai and to make them better.

The right price

How much you should expect to pay for a good bonsai really depends on supply, demand, and artistic quality. Obviously, supply and demand break down to how much you are willing to pay, and whether you can or can't live without the piece. Artistic quality is a little trickier. You can follow the guidelines here on what to look for in a good bonsai, but in the end it comes down to educating your eye over time. There is simply no substitute for looking at as many bonsai as you can. Go to public gardens, bonsai nurseries, shows and symposia, bonsai club meetings, and classes. See the great and the not so good, too. Unfortunately, there are a lot of not-so-good bonsai on sale these days. The majority are young nursery stock fresh out of their plastic pots, with a few branches cut off and a few copper wires twisted here and there. Although they are planted in bonsai pots, there is often little else to distinguish them as bonsai. If prices are modest for these "starter bonsai", they may be worth buying – many reputable firms offer very young bonsai at modest prices well suited to the beginner's abilities and budget. However, beware if the prices of these plants are high and the age in training does not correspond with the degree of developed design. You will probably see lots of bonsai in this category. But when you see some of the truly fine bonsai available today, you will know why there is such

a big difference in price. Once you have a little more visual experience to judge them by, these critiques and criteria will have more meaning.

When to buy

If you are new to bonsai and can only grow bonsai indoors, try to shop in early spring. Until you get the hang of indoor culture, this is the safest choice. Plants purchased in the fall will have an entire season of central heating ahead, during which time many may dry out, or succumb to pests; in extreme circumstances, they may die.

Outdoor growers have a wider latitude. If you are purchasing plants locally, you can buy at any time of the year. Keep in mind, however, that many trees sprout new leaves in early spring, and, until these leaves are fully expanded and mature, they are quite tender and easily damaged. Moving such bonsai, therefore, requires great care. Similarly, plants in bloom are difficult to move.

If you are taking a new plant home in your car, make sure that it is well watered. Don't stop at the roadside and leave your bonsai in a closed car to cook, and don't let the fan blow hot or cold air directly on your new plant. Whatever the season, all bonsai should be packed so that they do not slide or tip over during the ride home.

If you are planning to order bonsai by mail, arrange for delivery during the cooler months when plants are dormant, and will not get hot while they are being transported. In most areas, deliveries from late fall to early spring are safest. If you can afford to have your plant delivered overnight, so much the better: plants shipped in this way generally arrive in peak condition because they have not been sitting in a warm, dark box for several days. It is, clearly, difficult to get a large, spruce forest planted on a rock slab, for example, delivered. These large bonsai really should be transported by you, or through an arrangement with the nursery.

If this is your first purchase from a nursery, keep it small – one or, at most, two plants. When they arrive, unpack them immediately. If they have arrived undamaged, in good condition, and at the agreed time, future orders can be more ambitious. If there is a problem, contact the nursery immediately for a replacement or refund. Do not spend months trying to nurse a damaged plant back to health and then call with a complaint. It would be difficult to convince anyone that your plant had died because of shipping damage sustained six months before.

Importing bonsai

Inevitably, many bonsai fanciers eventually become plant collectors.

You soon become familiar with the catalogs of all of the nurseries specializing in plants for the connoisseur, and eventually you read about a plant that simply is not available anywhere in the country. At this point, many enthusiasts wish to try to import bonsai.

It is easier than you might think. The first step is to contact the US Department of Agriculture, APHIS, Federal Building, Hyattsville, MD 20782 for an Import Permit Application. Fill out this simple form and return it (there is no fee). A few weeks later, you will receive a packet that includes a permit valid for five years; mailing labels with your permit number; and plant lists enumerating:

- plants that cannot be imported because of potential disease or insect problems in the country of origin;
- noxious weeds that are barred;
- endangered plants banned from international trade (a special permit is required for these); and
- plants allowed entry without quarantine.

All plants bound for the US – including bonsai – must be shipped bare-root: free of soil, sand, moss, or leaf mold. That means they should be boxed and moist roots wrapped in one of the eleven approved packing materials such as peat moss or excelsior. Upon entry, the plants are checked at the nearest USDA Inspection Station before being released.

Zelkova serrata Zelkova
This eighty-year-old formal upright bonsai once belonged to the former Japanese Prime Minister Shigeru Yoshida, and is now part of the Kyuka-en Collection. The tree stands 38 inches high. Zelkovas are sun-loving, and should be kept out of the shade. It is also a good idea to prune the tips of the branches so that sunlight can reach right into the inner branches.

Chapter 4
The Care and Maintenance of Bonsai

Many newcomers to bonsai find the prospect of caring for and maintaining a collection rather daunting: after all, no two trees are the same – even trees from the same family can differ from one another in basic ways – and you could find yourself having to accommodate as many different care programs as you have trees in your collection. Caring for bonsai, however, is a logical process, based largely on common sense.

If, for example, you have a maple, a flowering cherry and a pine as the basis of your collection, you will soon find that you cannot give them all the same exposure, feeding, watering, and so on, but must allow for each variety's individual needs. What makes one tree different in needs from another, however, is fairly easy to sort out. In addition, you will find many similarities within each plant group, so that the time you spend accommodating each different species is likely to result in your being able to care for many more plants that fall into that category.

Learning these different and common factors is a never-ending process. It is worth persevering, though, since knowing even a smattering about bonsai care will also make you a better and more sensitive general gardener.

Juniperus rigida *Needle juniper*
This 230-year-old needle juniper – a stunning example of the driftwood style – has an interesting history in that for many years the present back was considered to be the front of the tree. The original front had crossed driftwood at the foot. It is only in the last five years, since the tree has been in the Oguchi Collection, that it has been reversed so that the more sculptured side of the trunk is the front.

Siting

The conditions each bonsai grower can give and the conditions each type of plant needs vary dramatically, so it is probably pointless to be too specific about where to site bonsai. Nor can siting be discussed without considering light and air, temperature and humidity, since they are interrelated to such an extent that one has an almost incalculable influence on the other.

The amount of moisture in the soil, as well as in the branches and leaves, can be directly attributed to the amount of sun a plant receives and the time of day it receives it. This means that the bonsai in its entirety is at the mercy of its site. Positioning, therefore, is not an isolated factor but rather represents the whole of the sum of the parts — the total picture of what light, temperature, humidity, and air circulation can produce.

Before going into specifics, it should be said that, in general, individual bonsai need as much light as is the requirement for the particular species during its growing season. Plants, in dormancy, kept at low (but above freezing) temperatures need less light.

Light

Light is one of the most important factors in encouraging proper growth. Bonsai must be exposed to light, either on shelves or other raised surfaces, for as much of the day as is appropriate to the particular species. There is, however, a big difference between light and direct sunshine. Strong, direct sunshine is made up of many things, including ultraviolet rays. These rays affect the growth of all plants.

Keeping the plant elevated gives protection from crawling insects and pests, and aids air circulation and viewing. While direct sunlight is necessary for growth and the plant's food-making process, it is also, paradoxically, a natural way to restrict excessive growth of bonsai material. Insufficient sunlight has the marked but undesirable effect of promoting the growth of weak foliage. If this is not corrected, it results in a weakened plant with shoots that are abnormally elongated and which will "burn" if suddenly exposed to full sun.

The sunlight in spring and fall is weaker than in summer, so bonsai can take exposure to it for longer periods. During summer, the drying effect of the sun itself and the increased heat, which dries up the remaining moisture in both soil and plant, make some relief from the sun necessary, especially by deciduous trees around midday and the early afternoon. If those trees are, in addition, in dark containers,

more of the heat is absorbed and this can cause damage, even death, to the roots. Some plants — like pines and a variety of flowering and fruiting plants such as pomegranates — can tolerate sunnier and drier conditions than most, but even they cannot take extremes. Others, including azaleas and rhododendrons, must have less.

Wind, too, is an important factor in the life of a plant. A gentle breeze helps discourage pests, disease, soot and dust.

Yet exposure to all the elements, from sun to rain and dew to cold, is an integral part of the healthy growth of most plants, with a few exceptions. Knowing what to provide for your plants is determined by the setting in which the plant is found naturally, and if those conditions are not available, in recreating them as closely as possible. You can provide

Private courtyard garden in Omiya.

This is an ideal garden for bonsai: the gravel acts as a mulch, while the tall trees and mid-height shrubs in the background act as both light filter and windbreak to protect the lower-growing varieties from harsh sunlight and sudden gusts.

shade where there is none, for example, by setting up a length of pierced cloth as an overhead screen for those plants that need light sun, and placing cardboard or firm plastic sheets covered with aluminum foil to reflect sunlight to those plants needing more sunlight. Alternatively, you could make a portable tilting shade screen, held on two wooden uprights, to protect your bonsai during the intense sunlight of a summer afternoon, removing it when it is not needed. Morning sun is far kinder, afternoon summer sun can be brutal.

It is very tempting to turn to the protection of the overhang of the eaves on the house or garage to protect bonsai, but where the overhang may be deeper than average, plants will not benefit from light rains, or they may be too shaded.

When a plant's light needs are not met, or if they are suddenly met, its growth and the direction of that growth are also changed. In weak light, plant cells elongate and leaves are spaced farther apart than usual. When in deep shade, branches will "stretch" toward the sun. Plants hidden under the eaves prove it, with their leggy limbs. In special cases – if you are trying to develop a windswept bonsai, for example – this general effect is desirable, although the weakening of the tree under such conditions is not. If you create an artificial source of light to produce a specific growth pattern, it should only be for a short period of time, and you should monitor plants carefully during that time.

In fact, as quickly becomes apparent, light has such a marked influence on bonsai that plants must be rotated a quarter turn every week or the bonsai will grow one-sided.

At the same time as you consider optima of light, you must also make decisions about how much water to give to them. With more sunlight comes the need for more water. If you work away from home all day, you may find your decision about the kinds of plants you can raise restricted by the conditions you can provide. An automatic watering timer or a drip irrigation system, readily available in most good nurseries, are options in these circumstances. Nothing, however, can take the place of good natural conditions and regular watering.

A common mistake is to switch bonsai from one set of conditions to another suddenly and frequently. Just because bonsai are so easily moved does not mean that they should be. Plants need to adjust to a change in conditions gradually. Sudden unwelcome changes can cause all manner of problems, including bud drop, flower or fruit fall, leaf drop, wilting, burned foliage, and death.

Soil

Soil supplies most of the moisture for plant growth and plant maintenance, as well as mineral elements for food production. At the same time, it acts as an anchor for the plant.

Soil should offer good water retention and drainage, and good food absorption potential. It should also be free from any germs that could cause disease and the eggs and larvae of potentially harmful insects; and its acidity/ alkalinity should be appropriate to the plants for which it is intended.

Soil should contain the qualities and substances that the intended plants need: a coarse texture, for instance, can speed growth and help an unhealthy plant to regain its vigor, while a finer texture can inhibit growth. Also, deciduous trees and broad-leafed evergreens require a richer soil with some sand, while conifers require more sand and a slightly poorer soil.

Traditionally, bonsaiists mixed their own soils, to "recipes" they found worked for their particular trees. For this reason, there are almost as many soil recipes for bonsai as there are enthusiasts. These, combined with a knowledge about, and a reasonable approximation of, the plant's native soil should make finding a viable mix for the plant a straightforward process.

Today, commercial soil mixes are readily available from bonsai nurseries. Most are based on a mixture of clay, topsoil or loam with humus content, and sand, with the addition of small quantities of nutritive substances. For quick-draining mixes, more sand is added; for richer mixes, more soil.

It is possible to produce homemade soil but it can take a long time. If you want to do this, the ingredients to have on hand are clay, pasteurized loam or topsoil (using fresh pasteurized topsoil avoids undesirables like bugs, diseases, and weeds), well-rotted manure, well-rotted leaf mold, and coarse sand or fine grit. Lay them all out in the sun to dry. At the same time, dispose of any insects in any of the materials.

Potting formulas are much like recipes. Many growers keep them secret but still more share them. The following are potting formulas used by Japanese growers. For conifers still in the development stage, they use five parts of clay, three of loam, and two of sand. For mature trees that have attained their final shape, they use six parts of clay, three of sand, and one of loam.

Deciduous trees and broad-leafed evergreens in development are happy with seven parts of loam, three of clay and one of leaf mold. After attaining their final shape, the plants thrive on two parts of loam, two of clay and one of sand.

Elms, zelkovas, and maples prefer seven parts of clay, three of loam and one of leaf mold, while bamboos and willows prefer three parts of loam, one of clay, and one of leaf mold. For flowering and fruiting trees the Japanese use eight parts of loam, two of clay, and one of leaf mold, while for rhododendrons and azaleas they mix seven parts of clay and three of chopped sphagnum or peat moss.

There is nothing sacred about any of these formulas, however. If you find a recipe works, use it. In some areas you may have to add more drainage material, in different geographical locations you may have to add more moisture-holding ingredients. A good basic recipe is a mix of two parts of loam, two of coarse sand or fine grit, and one of leaf mold or peat moss. Then, depending on the location and the plants used, the mix can be tailored to accommodate the tree more adequately.

In general, extra fine soil and very heavy clay do not meet the requirements of most plants. In fact, they can be the cause of problems. If compost is incorporated in the soil mix, it should be thoroughly decomposed and clean. Where peat moss is substituted, it, too, must be clean and should also be screened to eliminate large pieces of organic matter.

Clay

Clay is a popular subsoil used in bonsai. It must first be dried, broken, and screened into uniform granules of various sizes. When included in a potting mixture, these granules promote aeration of the soil by forming tiny open spaces which alternately fill with water when the soil is saturated and then with air as the water drains and the soil dries. This continuous interchange of air and water allows plant roots to "breathe". Thus the clay assists in supplying the bonsai with three basic needs: water, minerals, and oxygen. It is the clay that permits some bonsai to live in the sun with only one watering a day.

Granulated charcoal gives much the same airing action as clay pieces in the soil.

Loam

Unlike hard clay subsoils, which contain little organic matter or food value, rich loamy topsoils are used primarily to give bonsai a medium for their much-needed nourishment. Any good pasteurized garden loam or fibrous pre-packed loam – rubbed between your hands until it is granular – is acceptable.

Acer palmatum *Japanese maple* *Japanese maples are classic bonsai subjects, with more than 250 cultivars from which to choose. All have brilliantly colored fall foliage, ranging from* *pale yellow, through shades of orange, red, and purple. In addition, some have startling spring foliage color, as here: this photograph was taken in Japan in May.*

Humus

Peat moss, peat humus, leaf mold, or chopped sphagnum moss are all used in bonsai soils to help hold moisture, add slowly decaying humus to the mix, and to provide the acidity some plants need. Peat moss and sphagnum moss should always be dampened before use and should be clean.

Topsoil

When you use pasteurized topsoil, you must replace the missing natural ingredients by adding humus in the form of dried and sifted leaf mold or compost. Generally only a very small amount is necessary, since humus can be considered a growth stimulant, too growth-encouraging for dwarfed plants. For heavy feeders such as willows and the fruiting and flowering plants, however, it is a good idea to include as much as 25 percent in the potting mix.

Sand

Generally speaking, about $33\frac{1}{3}$ percent of a soil mix for evergreens and 10–15 percent for flowering plants and broad-leafed trees should be coarse sand. Sandy soil readily admits air and the spaces created in the soil by the presence of sand retain water in the same way as holes in a sponge. Once the soil is saturated with water, the air in the spaces is pushed out. Then, as the water is gradually drained by gravity it is again replenished by fresh air. This is an ongoing cycle that the bonsai must have if it is to grow. Sand is the basis for the process.

A granular soil also retains water and helps prevent the root hairs from drying, even when the spaces in the soil are completely devoid of moisture.

Roughly shaped sand grains are better than finely rounded sand. The angularity and roughness of sand stimulates the branching of fibrous roots, which enables the root to make its way through the soil. Roots naturally tend to expand radially outward; that is they grow to an outside wall and, once there, grow around and around it. This eventually weakens the root system, causing pot-bound and girdling conditions to develop. Coarse sand causes roots to change direction, which in turn encourages them to branch and to infiltrate the soil in the pot more thoroughly. Without a well-branched root system, good ramification and dense leafiness cannot develop above ground since the two systems mutually support and promote one another.

A word of caution: never use beach or aquarium sand. Both are too small and regularly shaped, and beach sand in addition is salty, which would mean death to roots. If you are buying sand from a builder's yard, check for salt or strong chemicals before use.

Soil sifting

Many Japanese growers use screens of various sizes set inside one another to sift their soils to an appropriate consistency. To do this, you will need four screens fitted with $\frac{1}{2}$ inch, $\frac{1}{4}$ inch, $\frac{1}{8}$ inch and $\frac{1}{16}$ inch wire. Stack them one on top of the other – the $\frac{1}{2}$ inch on top. Put a scoopful of soil on the top screen, then shake the whole stack back and forth until the soil has dropped through all four screens. Store the four grades separately in containers with lids and handles and keep in a dry place.

Throw the clods of soil that fall through the smallest screen on the compost pile since they will clog the root pores, and reserve the biggest particles for your very largest bonsai containers. Clods of clay should go in a shallow tub where they can be crushed to a finer consistency. The soil that remains on top is the one to use for the bottom-most layer in a bonsai container, with the soil in the second screen just above that. Mix the soils from the bottom two together and use them as the main potting soil mixture.

Substitute soils

The commercial potting soils now available at garden and hardware stores, as well as supermarkets, are ideal for beginners to bonsai. This packaged soil, guaranteed sterile, may also suit other bonsai enthusiasts who do not have the time or the space to start a soil mix from scratch.

This product should still be dried and sifted before use and, since it rarely includes clay, a substitute should be added along with an appropriate amount of sand. Since these commercial mixes also usually lack compost, it may be necessary to supplement the regimen of the bonsai planted in them with an application of liquid fertilizer about once a month.

Mulch

Oak leaf mold is a wonderful mulch. Homemade mulch or compost should be sterilized with boiling water to kill any insects and fungus which may be present, and coarse particles should be sifted out.

Temperature

A bonsai is a plant. A dwarfed plant it is true, but a plant – more often than not a tree or shrub – none the less. Most bonsai, therefore, live outdoors and are brought inside only for special occasions.

One of the problems that even a brief period of indoor living for a bonsai accustomed to living outdoors presents is heat. Temperatures in a home are much warmer than those an "outdoor" bonsai is used to. Even within a single home, these temperatures can vary widely from room to room and from season to season. Ventilation, too, can differ from room to room.

For the health of the bonsai, it generally should not remain indoors for more than a few hours at a time. If the room in which it will stay is cold or cool, it may be able to remain safely indoors for a full 24 hours, but ordinarily a very short time inside is best, especially in winter. In spring,

the best time for a brief indoor hiatus is just before or after the new shoots have hardened, and in fall, the bonsai can come in before the new growth has hardened off. Summer is no more critical than winter – in fact, less so. Just apply the same 24 hour rule. The temptation is to bring in a bonsai or two whenever the fancy takes hold or when guests are due. But it is not necessarily good for your bonsai.

Fortunately, most bonsaiists eventually have a variety of trees so they can usually choose one or two for temporary indoor display, or they have a collection of indoor bonsai which lives inside all the time (see Chapter 7). In this way the trauma of temporary change can be minimized by confining it to a once-a-season experience per outdoor tree, a situation which most healthy bonsai can deal with.

Outdoors, the tree can enjoy a place in the sun or semi-shade, whichever is appropriate. A sheltered corner can tame strong wind gusts into breezes. A shelf or table on which the bonsai can stand well above ground is mandatory for keeping crawling pests and insects from the trees. Open air is also required – close proximity to a heat-radiating wall can be devastating.

Natural weather conditions are necessary for the proper development of bonsai, but as in anything extremes can be fatal. If temperatures threaten to be abnormally high for even a day or two – never mind a heatwave – then you should make arrangements to bring the trees into a more temperate range for that period. Increased watering may have to be part of the program, too, both to keep the temperature of the tree down and to prevent the soil from drying out.

Storms can wreak havoc with bonsai, throwing over pots and trees alike. If possible, give them extra protection during high, gusty winds, and heavy rain.

Watering bonsai

Without water – and the closely related humidity – there would be no bonsai to care for. Water is the avenue by which moisture and nutrients are provided to the tree. It is the cleanser of leaves, the moistener of roots and soil, and its presence helps to raise the humidity around those trees that need a higher humidity than most. It also helps to settle both soil and roots in the container, especially after potting and repotting. With the limited amount of available soil, and no other source of moisture into which the tree can tap, rain and dew, augmented by watering, assume an even greater importance.

It is important to exercise care when watering, however, since with overwatering plants grow leggy and weak and invite disease. You should therefore plan carefully the number of times a bonsai is watered per day and the schedule it is on during any given season.

Watering is only appropriate when the dryness of the soil and the state of the leaves dictate its use. After root pruning, for example, there will be fresh soil into which new roots have not yet grown. That soil will dry more slowly because there are no roots present to absorb moisture. This is the time for great care in watering procedures. Due to the potential shock to newly pruned roots and their inability to take in as much water as usual, watering must be curtailed in order initially to prevent the tree from wilting. As new roots grow into the soil, the tree's water needs will increase and get back to normal.

There are some bonsaiists who provide their trees with distilled tap water; others go still further and keep goldfish in the water to provide small amounts of fertilizer; still others try to save rainwater for their trees since so many municipal drinking water supplies now contain chlorine and other chemicals (see also p. 116). It is up to you to decide which of these is the most suitable option for your collection.

Watering should be a gentle experience for bonsai, with a fine, even spray applied from overhead, geared to keep soil, mosses, and ground covers firmly planted, rather than wash them away. Traditional Japanese watering cans for bonsai, usually made of copper, are now widely available in the West. These have very long necks so that you can reach all the trees in a collection easily, and so that sufficient pressure builds up to force the water through the very fine nozzle. Initially at least, however, a fine spray rosette on the end of a watering can spout or hose will be adequate.

If the soil surface is unusually dry, it may not be able to accept water readily, so the drops will roll off the soil rather than sink in. To counteract this, immerse the tree, still in its pot, in a shallow dish holding a few inches of tepid water, barely reaching the rim of the bonsai container. When the soil darkens, the watering is complete. Wait until the water stops draining from the holes then water thoroughly from the top, concentrating water first around the base of the trunk, then sprinkling the rest of the soil from above. Finally syringe the trunk, branches, and leaves.

How to water bonsai

A *If the soil surface is very dry, immerse the whole container so that water is absorbed through the drainage holes into the rootball. Then, water from above. Always try to avoid watering in brilliant sunshine which may dry the surface of the soil before the water has time to reach all parts of the container, and which can result in burnt foliage.*

B *More bonsai die from lack of water than for any other reason. Use a fine rosette on the watering can, and hold it far enough above the container to reduce the speed of flow to a steady stream. Repeat two or three times, to insure that water penetrates as far as the rootball. Any excess will drain through the holes at the bottom of the container.*

During rainy weather, and in early spring when so many bonsai are either potted or repotted, you may only need to water your bonsai once or twice a week. This may increase to between one and four times a day during the heat of the summer. Once you have watered all your trees, go back to the beginning and start all over again, watering each tree until the water runs out the drainage holes. From spring to early summer, when your plants are in the middle of their growth spurt, watering should diminish to prevent rapid growth.

It helps to be observant. If you have a wide variety of trees in your collection, it will soon become obvious that some of the large-leafed trees and a few needled varieties, including the fruits and maples, beeches and bald cypresses, wisterias and willows, cedars and ivies, and others, need more water than, for instance, pines. For those heavy drinkers, provide a shallow dish filled with water. By the end of one day it will be empty and you should fill it again. Allow the pot to sit in a basin of water until the soil volume is wet – but not all day and not continuously. You will also notice that young plants absorb more water than older trees, and that plantings on rocks require even more than young trees.

Sometimes – it can be for any number of reasons – a tree undergoes a trauma that includes exceedingly dry conditions. Its leaves may droop and curl up, they may even drop. In such cases, you should initiate a program of very gradual watering to bring the tree back to its original condition. Do this by placing the tree temporarily in the shade. Every few hours give it a little more water until it is taking its normal allocation. Mist foliage every morning when the soil is watered and again later in the day. Keep the tree in a semi-shady, protected environment until it is back to normal.

Foliar watering is almost as important as basal watering. Aphids, red spider mites, soot, dust, and more are removed from the leaves by regular watering to allow photosynthesis to proceed unhampered. The leaves are also refreshed, especially in high midsummer temperatures. They benefit from a syringing in early morning with water that is approximately the same temperature as the atmosphere around them.

Yet another factor in the moisture story is that of humidity. During the heat of the summer, your bonsai plants will benefit enormously if you water the entire area – benches, rear wall, ground or paving stones, fence, grass – in short, everything that could possibly raise the humidity level even a little.

Fertilizing

Fertilizing is the controlled feeding of plants. It is a regular and pivotal part of any horticultural health program, more so for bonsai because they cannot thrust out their roots in the direction of nutrients and other sources of nourishment to keep them growing. You must provide for their health.

It is important to know approximately, if not exactly, the variety, age, condition, and normal growth patterns of the plant in question. Data can vary widely from bonsai to bonsai and this has a major influence on the feeding program you adopt. In planning such a program, you should take these general points into account:

- Feeding begins in spring and stops in fall, with food applied only during active growing periods.
- After transplanting, fertilization is held in abeyance for one to two months.
- A complete feeding once a month or a smaller feeding twice a month is more than adequate for most trees.
- Some plants need a special mix of fertilizer for acid lovers. For them, a food high in iron is needed, whereas for most other fruiting, berrying, flowering, and coning material, a food based on bonemeal and cottonseed meal is appropriate.
- If the soil appears to be too acidic, a little wood ash, horticultural lime or charcoal will "sweeten" it.
- Several obvious leaf problems, such as yellowing, discoloration or spotting, can be a direct result of a shortage of nutrients in the bonsai's diet. A feeding with a complete fertilizer that has all the trace elements may help in arresting, then eliminating, the problem.

There is an enormous difference between withholding growth stimulants and starving a plant. Bonsai, like every other living thing, need to be fed, but there is a finer line than normal between solid nourishment and overfeeding for bonsai.

The most important nutrients taken up by plants are nitrogen, phosphorus and potash, and most proprietary brands of fertilizer supply these nutrients in a ratio of approximately 5:3:2. Nitrogen promotes the growth of green leaves, phosphorus the growth of flowers and fruit, and potash the development of a healthy root system, although all are necessary, and all promote other factors in the overall health of plants.

Amount

A crucial fact to know about fertilizing any plants is that "less is more". Beware of the temptation to err on the generous side; especially in the case of bonsai, you can not only kill with kindness but cause an overstimulation of growth. Remember that technically plants make their own food. In sunlight, they combine the necessary elements from air and water and, in combination with the nutrients absorbed by their roots, carry on photosynthesis, the making of food. In considering the controlled rate of growth you want to maintain with bonsai, great care should be exercised where adding nutrients or fertilizers to their diet is concerned. Being safe rather than sorry may mean altering the manufacturer's recommended application to suit the particular situation on hand.

Considering the restricted growth space for bonsai roots, less concentrated, more frequent feedings are better than label-recommended doses. Whether the fertilizer is liquid or powder, dilute or dissolve it in water at a third to no more than half the recommended rate.

A point worthy of special note concerns a tree that is not in good health. Unless the symptoms indicate that the condition is the result of a nutrient deficiency feeding a weakened plant usually worsens its condition.

The food itself

Chemical fertilizers are fast acting and do not enhance the texture of the soil. Organic fertilizers, including cottonseed meal, blood meal, bonemeal, and composted animal manures, act more slowly, and are favored by most bonsaiists.

Prunus subhirtella
Higan flowering cherry
This flowering cherry was trained as a bonsai at the Brooklyn Botanic Garden by Frank Okamura. The principal disadvantage of working with many of the flowering cherries is that their beautiful blossom – which ranges in color from almost white with the faintest hint of pink, as here, through pale pink to deep pink – lasts for a very short time, after which the trees can appear uninteresting. They are, however, easy to cultivate, and many people find the glory of the spring blossom more than adequate compensation.

Combinations of these fertilizers can be applied in different ways, including as a dust and a liquid. To make a dust fertilizer, mix two parts of cottonseed meal with one part blood meal in a dry clean container with an airtight lid. Put a small portion of the fertilizer in the corners of the pot and allow it to be slowly distributed over the bottom surface of the container as water reaches it.

The best liquid fertilizers to use are fish emulsion, which comes ready for use with directions on the bottle, and manure tea, which is homemade. Mix one part of dried manure with ten parts of water. Allow the manure to steep for one month during the summer or for three months in winter so that it is fully fermented. Use only the clear liquid on top, diluted, and store it in an airtight container.

Manure tea can be used on flowering and fruiting trees in spring when the new buds appear. Give two or three applications within a few days of each other. Then, as the leaves open, water once a week. In summer, use manure tea once a week, and in fall give two or three strong applications at intervals of a few days before dormancy sets in. Feeding is not necessary in winter.

Various kinds of manure can bring back the green to pale leaves: the most commonly used vegetable manures are cottonseed or soybean meal; animal manures include waste from fish, cattle, horses, and chickens.

Manure can also be pounded into a powder and sprinkled over the soil at the edge of a pot or mixed into a paste by adding water to powdered manure. Let it mature for a while until it emits a strong odor. Make small balls about 1 inch in diameter with a melon ball cutter and push them into the corners of the pot. Paste is especially good for rock plantings because it sticks to the rock.

There are also materials that can be incorporated at the time of soil mixing that accomplish much in the way of nutrition. To increase the recognized effects of the materials in soil such as sand, sphagnum moss, perlite or grit, for instance, add peat moss, peat humus, or leaf mold.

To exaggerate specific effects, you can add compost – a mix of decayed or partially decayed organic matter created from grass cuttings, leaves, chemical-free organic waste such as carrot tops and potato peel, lettuce leaves, tea leaves (not bags), crushed egg shells, fruit peel and skins, manure, and the like. These ingredients should be allowed to decompose naturally. In as short a time as two or three months, or as long as a year, compost will result from the breakdown of these materials due to bacterial action. If everything is first broken up into small pieces, the process will be that much faster.

General guidelines

It is possible to generalize to a certain extent. The fertilization program that many bonsaiists feel comfortable with starts in early spring with a diluted feeding of every bonsai that has not been repotted and that might be root bound.

LEFT AND OPPOSITE:
Chaenomeles × superba
"Corallina" Flowering quince
This thirty-year-old windswept bonsai measures 23 × 21 inches, by 21 inches high overall. One of several flowering quince hybrids, this has brilliant red flowers and bright yellow anthers; others range from bright orange-red, through rose-pink to rich deep red. All are among the most suitable flowering species to train as bonsai since their flowers are small, and do not look at all incongruous on a miniature planting. This bonsai follows the general "rule" that red-flowering plants look their best in basic
brown pots, in this case a hexagonal, unglazed, lipped style, which is 4 inches high. The quinces are native to China, although they are very common in Japanese bonsai, and are suitable for training in many styles.

Saplings and new plants may need additional feedings during the late spring and early summer growth spurt, and again in summer after the new growth has hardened. One or two feedings are appropriate in fall after the leaves begin to fall.

Again, generally speaking, trees with needles do not feed as heavily as leafed trees, while flowering and fruiting trees are the heaviest feeders of all. The latter can, however, benefit from weekly, very diluted feedings during budding and fruit formation.

A growing number of bonsaiists alternate a variety of fertilizers, recognizing that any one regime used repeatedly could lose its effectiveness. And some bonsaiists have beautiful and diverse collections which they have never fertilized at all.

Emergency treatment

As careful as you are, emergencies do happen and it is best to be prepared. Whatever the cause, pick up the pieces, salvage whatever is salvageable and concern yourself with the affected plants.

If the tree is sick or weakened in any way, remove it gently from its container. If it is wired into a now broken container, carefully untwist the wires, freeing the root system. Slowly comb out the roots that edge the rootball. Then check the rootball itself. The likelihood is that the rootball will be intact and that pruning any broken or crushed roots along the edges will take only a few minutes. Try to keep the roots moist until the tree is repotted. Once the tree is in its new container, place it carefully in semi-shade.

If the trunk or any of the branches is damaged, clean off the broken portions as close to a node as possible and put the tree into a holding bed. When the trunk has been severely damaged, for example, if the apex has been severed, consider creating a jin at the first appropriate opportunity (see pp. 79–81). If the upper portion has been only partially severed, complete the separation, using jin techniques if a jin is appropriate.

When you suspect disease or pests are the problem, remove the soil and plant the bonsai in pure clean sand in semi-shade, taking the proper organic (or chemical, if necessary) steps to eliminate the source. Do not fertilize.

If a bonsai tree suddenly wilts even though its care has been correct, put it in a shady, draft-free area for the day. Follow the same watering procedures it had been receiving, neither increasing nor decreasing the quantity. It is possible that the tree will have recovered by evening. In that case, immediately place it back in its original position and continue the same treatment. Don't wait until a day or two have passed – it will quickly become accustomed to shade and may suffer further when you return it to the sun.

Pests and diseases

Since it is undoubtedly true that avoiding trouble is easier than getting rid of it, it is fortunate that any good bonsai maintenance program automatically includes many "helpers" to assist in keeping trees pest and disease free.

The forceful spraying of foliage, for instance, is just what the tree needs to get rid of many types of aphids and spider mites. Growing the trees on a raised platform makes it easier to spot those creatures that could do them harm and makes taking emergency steps that much easier. The individual close attention that every tree gets each day when it is watered is perhaps the single most powerful preventive of all.

Insects, pests, and diseases can cause everything from premature leaf or fruit fall to withering of the tree and ultimate death. The unchecked infestation of one tree in a collection presents a real problem, since that malady can easily spread to other trees.

If your display tables are placed on grass or soil, sprinkle a mixture of equal parts of borax and sugar to attract then do away with pests. When chemical treatment is necessary, use the smallest amount of insecticide possible. Generally try to find an organic solution to a problem.

Probably the most damaging disease is *root decay*. This is caused by a variety of factors, including a soil mixture that provides poor drainage, a soil mixture that provides poor water retention, transplanting at an inappropriate time, and too much water after transplanting. To save the tree, transplant it immediately, pruning affected roots up to solid, healthy tissue.

Aphids secrete a sticky substance called "honeydew", which draws ants from far and wide. Aphids, in turn, are often carried by ants from plant to plant. In large part, therefore, ants can be controled by keeping the aphid population off the bonsai trees and aphids can be controled by keeping the ant population from the collection. It helps to take care of the area immediately surrounding the bonsai display tables. One solution is to put the legs of your bonsai tables in buckets filled with water and an insecticide.

Slugs and snails are easy to spot and can be controled with traps filled with poison. Worms and caterpillars can be plucked by hand. If you have to resort to chemical sprays, make sure that the soil in the container has been thoroughly drenched with plain water first and reduce the possibility of burning the trees by spraying on a cloudy, cool day.

One of the most common and dangerous pests is the *spider mite*. Telltale symptoms of its presence are a paling of the foliage color, which becomes speckled, turns yellow or gray, and eventually browns. Isolate the infested tree and treat with pyrethrum and nicotine or dusting sulfur. The recuperation period can be long: it may be months before the tree is completely back to its normal healthy state.

Tough to control, *scale insects* can be black or brown and look like tiny stationary oyster shells on the stems or undersides of leaves. They can be kept away with a tar oil spray when dormant or in early spring before bud break. Pick them off as you see them.

Sooty mold is a fungal growth that covers the leaves with a black dust and looks terrible. Aphids, scale, and other small insects leave secretions on the leaves that develop mold and turn black. To discourage its growth, spray with dormant oil in late winter/early spring. If it appears after leaves have sprouted, spray both upper and lower sides of the leaves with soap and water. Also spray the leaves of any garden trees overhanging the bonsai collection.

Mildew attacks young leaves and branches, making them look as though they have been sprinkled with flour. An improvement in air circulation and sun should help. When it first appears, spray the affected tree with bordeaux mixture. In fall, collect and burn the leaves.

Rust creates tiny grains of various colors that grow on new leaves and woody growth. It is at its prime in late spring and early summer. Catch it in the early stages of the disease and spray, then gather up and burn all fallen leaves.

Leaf spot produces gray, brown or black spots on leaves, new growth, branches and fruits, especially on deciduous trees. A bordeaux mixture spray will help, as will gathering all leaves, fruits and prunings from the trees in fall.

Borers, which can kill a tree, leave a very obvious trail of slime on the woody parts of trees and near the holes they bore. An affected tree must be injected with nicotine or pyrethrum directly in the borer's holes. Use a sterile syringe and needle for this, and then seal the hole with either paraffin wax or clay.

Earthworms should be discouraged from bonsai containers with the application of a moderate-strength pyrethrum solution.

Citrus aurantium *Orange Oranges are the hardiest citrus species, needing a minimum temperature of 55°F for six months after flowering in spring for fruits to ripen. Although prone to frost damage, they relish summers outside. Pests can be a problem with fruit trees – as can birds which will strip fruits and berries – but oranges are no more prone than other fruits. This photograph was taken in Kyuka-en.*

Mealy bugs look like tiny puffs of cottonwool. The time-honored method of removing them is to touch each one with a cottonbud dipped in rubbing alcohol.

Nematodes attack the roots, sapping the tree of energy and eventually causing death. If you suspect nematodes are present, replace the soil with fresh soil, and before repotting prune all the swellings from the roots, submerge the remaining roots in a lime solution for about 10 to 15 minutes and repot.

Rabbits and *mice* may prune your trees uninvited. A very taut wire screen may be necessary to protect the trees at the level closest to the ground. Mice and rabbits are inclined to snuggle in with bonsai during the winter when the bonsai are in their cold-frames or garden beds. Screening firmly nailed around the area helps keep them away.

Birds have been known to snatch moss from the soil and fruits from the branches of bonsai.

Winter protection

Winter presents a challenging set of circumstances for the bonsaiist and his or her bonsai. It is the one season in which the trees are not overtly growing and in many parts of the world are dormant.

The needs of the bonsai must be anticipated in preparation for the cold months to come. Exposure to the extremes of winter should be gradual before the trees are finally stored for overwintering. If excessive, remove some of the ground covers. Plant these in separate containers in your winter storage area. Lightly scratch the surface of the soil to insure that moisture will penetrate easily.

The specific requirements vary according to where you live. In areas where freezing temperatures and snow are the order of the winter's day, you can choose between storage in a pit, a shelter, a cold basement, an unheated room or shed, an unheated garage or outbuilding, a cold-frame or a specially prepared bed.

In areas where the ground freezes at night but thaws during the day, a protected shelter that provides free air circulation is sufficient. The hardier specimens, those that can survive the prevailing cold extremes, may do well in a heavily mulched box or raised bed with the container submerged in a thick layer of soil. If night temperatures do not dip below freezing, little special treatment is required.

Exceptional winters do present themselves, however, so it is better to be well prepared than not. Besides preserving the health of the tree, proper winter care of bonsai will help

to insure that their containers remain in one piece and that the texture of the soil is not changed by alternating freezing and warming temperatures.

If winter generally produces a consistent stretch of nights with temperatures dropping below about 35°F, special preparations for cold conditions are necessary. The exact time for carrying out those plans varies from area to area. If special attention is needed even for a short time, hardy bonsai must be "conditioned", that is, exposed to cold temperatures and frost for several short periods before being placed in their new winter environment.

The verified winter hardiness of plants is one of the most important criteria in deciding what your course of action should be. Information about hardiness zones and specific plants is given on pp. 120–41. The point to remember is that these hardiness zones reflect air temperature. Soil temperatures must be considered, too, however. Your goal is to create a situation where both roots and top growth are kept in even temperatures, cold enough to maintain dormancy yet not so cold that injury results. A prime factor is to have the collection where it is visible, accessible, close

Cedrus atlantica 'Glauca'
Blue Atlas cedar
This cascade bonsai was created thirty years ago, and it is estimated to be about forty-five years old. Evergreen, it has a pale gray bark and blue-gray foliage. Originating in the Atlas Mountains of north Africa, this is one of the most common cultivars grown in Europe and ideal for bonsai, although it does need protection from cold winter winds. Snow is an excellent mulch for overwintering bonsai, keeping both plant and soil moist, well insulated and at a constant temperature.

to a source of water and protected from both wind and what is called "winter kill" – the killing or injuring of leaves, stems, and branches due to a freezing/thawing cycle which goes unstabilized.

One course of action is to dig a bed against the wall of a building, preferably east or north, well in advance of freezing temperatures. During the winter, the warmth from the heated building will help to prevent the soil from freezing and thawing repeatedly and the eastern exposure helps to curb the extreme temperature fluctuations you might expect with northern or western exposures. If this is not possible, a space to the east or north of a hedge or group of shrubs should still provide protection.

Plant the bonsai, pots and all, in the bed and mulch them with either leaves, pine needles, wood chips, or soil. (Hopefully, nature will supply her own singular kind of mulch – snow. Snow is the best insulator/moisturizer/temperature regulator of all. The most troublesome winters are the ones in which very little snow falls while temperatures seesaw up and down. A heavy blanket of snow moderates the effect of such instability.)

Build a windbreak of any material that will withstand winter winds and cold temperatures – closely woven nylon mesh, burlap, canvas, even plastic are all suitable – around the bed. Surround the bed with stakes driven into the ground, leaving about 3 feet of stake above ground, and attach the windbreak to it. If you need a more permanent barrier, bricks, cement blocks, marine plywood, and garden fencing are appropriate.

Building a cold-frame

Cold-frames are an easily assembled form of storage area. Either buy one in kit form, or make your own. Look for a well caulked but discarded window and build the cold-frame to fit its size. Measure the ground dimensions created after placing the window at an angle steep enough for rain and snow to drain off easily and tall enough to accommodate the tallest bonsai in the collection. Then add another 6 inches to the depth.

Dig a pit facing east or north 12–18 inches below the soil line and spread about 4 inches of small pebbles across the bottom for drainage. Carefully measure the front, back, and sides of the window, then cut marine plywood to size. Hinge the back of the window to the back of the box so the window can be opened easily for access. Cut rigid polystyrene insulation to fit each side, and fasten it inside the plywood sides. Then, butt the corners tightly up against each other to eliminate potential drafts and fasten together. Once the shell is together, lower it carefully into the pit, back-filling round the outer edges of the shell with the soil removed from the hole.

Place a long hook in the center front of the window and drive a thick stake in the ground behind the cold-frame or on the house. Fasten a cup or eye hook to receive the hook onto this for keeping the top of the cold-frame open as plants are placed in and taken from it.

Before finally putting your bonsai in winter storage, spray the leaves and needles of the broad-leafed evergreens and conifers with an anti-desiccant to prevent their drying out. Do this twice on a day when the temperature is over 40°F. Deciduous trees do not need this treatment, since they will drop their leaves.

Care during dormancy

During dormancy, bonsai are really "resting", or spending a sufficient amount of time as dormant plants so they will have the energy to carry on adequate growth, coning, flowering, and fruiting when dormancy passes. Without this period the plants weaken.

It is during this period, too, that careful scrutiny of each tree, especially the deciduous varieties, is relatively easy. With no leaves to hide structural faults, deciduous trees can be re-evaluated. Make notes of any later changes you think will be necessary.

During dormancy, bonsai need no light if temperatures range between 32° and 42°F. To be sure that temperatures are maintained, place a few refrigerator thermometers that register the lowest readings in different parts of the storage area and make periodic checks.

Watering during dormancy should be kept to a minimum. With respiration down, moisture needs are also down. If the collection is kept outdoors and exposed to the elements, then rain and melted snow will provide all the moisture they need. If, however, your collection is in a dark garage, basement, shed or cold-frame, watering will prevent the soil from completely drying out so that when temperatures rise even temporarily, the roots have enough moisture to prevent dehydration.

In these enclosed environments, soil will tend to dry out faster than outdoors, so you should check the moisture in bonsai containers on a regular basis – every four days should be often enough. When temperatures rise outside, they will rise inside and when they do, any residual moisture will evaporate quickly. That is the time to water the soil of each tree lightly – but not enough to drench the plant or remain in the container long enough to become icy if the temperature falls.

It is not a good idea to overwinter bonsai in valuable containers. If your tree is in such a container, remove it and put it in a temporary container the same size and shape as its original, made from several sheets of extra-heavy aluminum foil, molded to exactly the same measurements as the original. In the bottom, cut identically placed drainage holes and put screening over them. As a precaution, sprinkle a light dusting of soil over the foil, then put the bonsai inside. Since most bonsai pots have feet or a rim to keep the bottom from directly touching the surface of the display stand, make a substitute from a thin strand of florist's foam around the bottom of the pot, or make "feet" and place them exactly where the container's feet are located. In the spring, the bonsai will go back into its proper pot without experiencing any change.

When winter ends, don't be too eager to bring your bonsai out and place them on their display tables: spring weather can be unpredictable. Check the weather forecasts and always err on the side of caution. When you do bring bonsai outside again, set them in semi-shade for a week and then gradually expose them to full light and sun. If there is a freeze after the bonsai are outside, quickly spray the plants both top and bottom as often as necessary to avoid thick ice crystals forming on the tree and on new growth. Injury may not be avoided but irreparable harm will be.

Vacations

Bonsai, like people, respond to change. What they do not like are surprises and sudden changes in circumstances for which they are not prepared.

There are several courses open to you when you go on vacation. First, a fellow bonsaiist or a gardening enthusiast might be willing to take charge in exchange for a reciprocated kindness. If this is not possible, during warm weather the bonsai should be placed in an area that offers more protection from sun and wind than normal. A sprinkler on a reliable timer is not a perfect alternative but it is feasible. Make sure that watering takes place early enough in the morning to stand the plants in good stead during the heat of the day, that the second watering takes place at an appropriate time later on, and that there is someone who will check on the bonsai periodically.

The situation to avoid is that of placing the bonsai under glass or plastic since, even with regulated watering, without regular observation they could easily suffer from heat damage, pest or disease damage, starvation, or any of a number of other conditions.

In winter, when the trees are in cold storage, they will only need looking at a couple of times a week. Keep a watering can at hand, and make sure your "caretaker" has access to running water.

Containers

Many experts have called the bonsai pot the closest thing to a picture frame that a tree can have. Its job, like that of a frame, is to show the bonsai in the best possible light. The characteristics of a good bonsai container include:

- adequate provision for drainage;
- frost resistance in the form of outwardly slanted sides as opposed to inwardly slanted sides;
- a shape and color that display the bonsai to its best advantage; and
- an unglazed interior.

Cedrus atlantica "*Glauca*"
Blue Atlas cedar
Removed from its overwintering position and back on display, the cascade-style blue Atlas cedar pictured on pp. 60–1, and its beautiful pot, can be clearly seen. It follows the conventions that evergreens look best in neutral brown pots, and that cascades need taller pots than most other styles so that the pot is not visually overpowered by the downward-sweeping trunk and branches. Hexagonal pots are softer in effect than other shapes – perfect for the tree's arching trunk and blue-gray foliage.

ABOVE AND ABOVE RIGHT:
Gyozan Nakano is considered one of the finest makers of bonsai pots working today. His shop is in Tokoname in Japan, which has been a site of potterymaking since ancient times and where most of the world's bonsai containers are still manufactured. Nakano's pots are slab-built, rather than hand-thrown, since this results in a stronger pot able to withstand many seasons of frost, and then fired in gas-fired kilns.

RIGHT: *Nakano makes pots commercially, but also produces special "one-offs" for selected customers, which he signs. Although there are still clay deposits in Tokoname, he chooses to work with a mixture of about half and half local and Chinese clays. Pottery factories are becoming more common in Japan, which has tended to push up the prices of pots by individual potters like Nakano, even if they are not produced as one-offs. Interestingly, however, potters are now working in the West, producing classically styled bonsai containers to rival some of the finest from Japan.*

Among the many suitable materials are ceramics, wood, cement, stoneware, earthenware, and porcelain, all of which may be glazed or unglazed.

Over the years, it has become traditional to select rather neutral shades of brown, gray and red for evergreens and the more colorful pots of green, blue, and white for deciduous trees. It has also long been recognized, for example, that flowering trees look good in blue, green, and deep purple pots. The exception to this is that trees and shrubs with red flowers look best in white pots. All of them look good in basic brown glazed or unglazed pots.

Fruiting trees can handle the competition of colored pots and certain traditions have developed around them. For instance, it is considered the norm to place trees with red fruit in white pots and trees with yellow or orange fruits in blue pots. Basic brown, again, is always correct.

Both evergreen and deciduous trees known for their highly colored foliage follow the norms, with almost any vibrant color looking well in green, red-leafed trees looking well in white, and yellow or orange looking well in blue containers. Again, the finishes can be either glazed or unglazed. Highly glazed black pots and oatmeal or butterscotch tones, while not common, can also be most effective.

Generally, the more mature and aged the bonsai, the plainer the container should be. The more delicate the tree, the lighter in color the container should be.

It is also important that the size relationship between bonsai and container is in harmony with the visual shape and weight of the tree.

Bonsai containers are available in almost every geometric shape. From square to rectangular, round to oval, from deep pots for cascades to square and round, they come in all sizes and variations. You can sometimes find nests of three or four sizes at prices reasonable enough to allow you to purchase a nest in anticipation of the growth and possible upgrading of a bonsai in training or the acquisition of other trees for those pots. Generally speaking, though, select the tree first and begin its training before buying a pot.

LEFT: *Nakano produces pots of all shapes and sizes from* mame *to "four-man lifting size", both glazed and unglazed, and in different colors, as the shelves of his workshop show. Generally, glazed pots tend to have a shorter lifespan than unglazed, so you may need to take this into account if you intend to spend a lot of money on a container. Choosing the right container is crucial, but remember that rules can be broken; if you are in any doubt, you cannot go wrong with a plain unglazed earth-color pot.*

Grooming

Little is said about grooming bonsai trees, probably because most bonsai receive much more care and attention than other trees of the same variety planted in the garden, and than most indoor plants.

There are factors that need special attention, however, certainly if you intend to show your bonsai in public. When on view, a bonsai must be neatly pruned. That may seem obvious, but there are residual effects of pruning that are not always taken into account by bonsaiists. For instance, major pruning scars should be healed and closely aligned with the trunk or branch. In some cases, a bit of muck – a loose mixture of clay and water (see p. 102) – can be rubbed on an obvious cut or scar to disguise it.

A tree on exhibition should have dead leaves, dead flowers, dried fruit and dead branches removed unless they are part of the esthetic composition. The soil should be well mossed and clean. The container should be clean, too, with no tiny pieces of compost or gravel or soil lingering on its surface. In addition, the bonsai should be displayed on a stand or base that is appropriate in style, color, shape, and height. Bases are now readily available in wood and lacquered finishes, bamboo and ceramics.

Mosses and lichens
There are functions for everything in bonsai and mosses and lichens, used as ground covers, are no exceptions. They of course look beautiful, covering the soil surface with green velvet or with gray-green shag, and they help retain water while holding the soil in the container. When not used for "conservation" purposes, they should be planted sparingly so that their effect is natural and they do not prevent water from reaching the soil.

There is a particular method of mossing a potted bonsai that will produce a smooth mat of deep green, with none of the lumpy growth that can be typical of piecing bits of moss together. With a sharp knife, slice the moss from its growing place taking as little soil as possible. Put this moss in a container lined with paper and water it lightly (it should be moist, but not wet). Remove most of the remaining soil from the moss using sharp scissors, pulling each little tuft away from the larger piece.

Prepare the surface soil in the bonsai pot by scratching it to roughen it up. With long-handled tweezers, start inserting each tuft of moss close to, but not against, the trunk. Work out and away from the trunk until you have the look you want, then brush off most of the tufts. Sprinkle dry soil over the moss and press the moss down with a flat spatula or small trowel. Mist gently two or three times and the soil will settle down between the tufts.

Alternatively, you can use dried moss. Gather it, then place it in the shade for a few days until it is dry. Put it through a fine strainer – a sieve will do – to crumble it. Mix the particles with some soil and spread it over the bonsai soil in the pot, making a thin, even layer. Press it down with a flat spatula or small trowel and gently mist continually until the soft green moss begins to grow.

Laying moss and ground covers

1 *Moss can be found in the cracks between paving stones, or growing on rough stones. (Woodland moss is too tall for bonsai.) Use your fingers or a pair of tweezers to insert the tufts into the surface of the soil, and press it down with your fingers.*

2 *If you are in any doubt as to whether the moss is going to "take", secure it temporarily with copper wire, bent into hairpin shapes. The tree in the background has been mossed only a few weeks and is greening up well.*

Along with the growth of a healthy crop of moss often comes the appearance of a silver fungus around the soil line at the trunk of the tree. This is a sign of a healthily growing bonsai. The fungus develops as the moss takes hold and it cannot be artificially implanted.

In the heat of the summer, moss may turn brown. Do not despair – it means the bonsai is getting the water it needs. As soon as cooler temperatures and higher humidity return, so will the green velvet.

When you need more moss, sprinkle the shredded moss particles you have stored in an airtight jar on the watered surface of the soil and watch it green up.

Chaenomeles × superba "Corallina" Flowering quince A close-up of the base of the trunk of the flowering quince pictured on pp. 56–7. A lush carpet of green moss is particularly effective where the tree's roots are visible, as here. The club mosses (Selaginella), and many of the low-growing species such as Crassula spp., heathers (Erica spp.), and sedges (Carex sp.), generally available as rock-garden or "alpine" plants, are also suitable ground-cover plants. A good covering of moss or other low-growing plants may well be moisture-retaining, so your bonsai will probably need less frequent watering. Remember, too, to avoid letting the moss grow up the tree trunk, since here it could cause rot to set in.

Chapter 5
Creating Bonsai

Creating what the world will recognize as a beautiful bonsai and, more importantly, what you will appreciate as a growing, definitive expression of your own, is a challenge that bonsaiists have accepted for hundreds of years, refining the style and skill that elevates bonsai from a craft to an art.

Bonsai is something of a paradox: precise and specific steps are needed to get it started, yet it depends on an intensely personal interpretation of life and nature.

Over the centuries a number of bonsai styles have evolved. These styles come directly from nature and exist because the conditions in which plants live vary widely, and so have produced many different but specific physical characteristics. It is those characteristics that bonsaiists have chosen to interpret and reproduce in their own environments so that they can enjoy them at their leisure.

In this chapter, the formal classifications of style are outlined, as are the time-honored techniques of shaping plants into those styles. These techniques are merely refinements of those you probably use already in your garden. Finally, the steps to take in potting and repotting that material are discussed.

Pinus parviflora *Japanese white pine*
This windswept bonsai from the Mansei-en Collection, Japan, is planted in a rock-shaped brown unglazed pot, traditionally used for slanted and cascade styles, in addition to windswept plantings. Bonsai in this style should, as here, give the impression of a tree buffeted by strong directional winds. Any additional plants in the composition, to appear natural, should also show this directional lean.

Bonsai sizes

Bonsai are classified according to both size and style, so that both practitioners and viewers have a method of reference. There are four common sizes.

Large bonsai are the greatest acceptable size. These range from about 26 inches to 4 feet maximum height, excluding the pot. The Japanese refer to large bonsai as a "two man", "three man" or "four man" lifting size. Generally, they are used as decoration in a garden, on a porch, or inside an appropriately scaled building.

Medium bonsai are the size that a person of average build can easily move from one place to another, their height generally agreed to be from about 12–26 inches. This is probably the most effective and practical size to develop and collect, and for the Japanese, it is the most appropriate size for their homes.

Next come the *small*, "one hand" lifting size, bonsai. Depending on the style, this is a tree of about 7–12 inches and is the most popular size among American bonsai enthusiasts. It excludes the clinging-to-rock style.

The smallest of all are the *mame* (pronounced "mahmay") or baby bonsai. These are a diminutive 7 inches or less in height and they can easily sit in the palm of one hand. In fact, two or three can sit in the palm of one hand at one time if they are small enough. This size attracts a lot of interest, but there are problems with *mame*, including the difficulty in shaping such small material into artistic bonsai. And such bonsai – in their minuscule containers – need almost constant watering.

Bonsai styles

No matter what size a bonsai is, it fits into a category that stems from one of five basic styles. These styles were developed from the direct relationship between the angle that the bonsai's main trunk makes with its container's horizontal rim. An accomplished bonsaiist will take one of these styles as a starting point only, and look beyond it, to create a personal expression of his or her own.

Bonsai styles are very specific. A *formal upright* bonsai, which is perhaps the most difficult style to achieve, has a straight trunk with a natural taper from its wider base to its narrower top. Branches are symmetrically spaced so that they are balanced when viewed from any direction. About

Miscanthus *sp. Water grass*
Proof that almost all plants are suitable for bonsai, this water grass forms part of the Sudo Collection in Japan. A forest style planting, this occupies a shallow, round unglazed lipped container, which in turn is placed on a highly polished wooden slab. The fresh green leaves, which arch as they reach upward, and upright stems rustle with the slightest breeze. This bonsai is also heavily mossed. Arundinaria spp. (bamboo) is often used in a similar way in Japan, and certainly enhances the oriental feel of any collection. The plant is on display, with a scroll depicting fish swimming upstream, at the Yonan-so Hotel, Utsunomiya.

one-third of the trunk is visible from the front, either from the base to the first branch or cumulatively, as seen through the tracery of its branches. Generally, the placement of branches follows a pattern. The first, and the heaviest and longest, almost makes a right angle to the trunk. The second branch directly opposes the first branch and is higher on the trunk. The tip of the bonsai has a slight curve, to lean forward to "look at the viewer". (This concept comes from traditional Japanese flower arranging, where it is important that the arrangement "looks at" the viewer, rather than leaning toward the ground or sky. The stance of the viewer in relation to the tree is particularly important in bonsai.) The top of the bonsai is so full and tightly ramified that it is difficult to see its internal structure through the mass of foliage.

The *informal upright* bonsai has a straight or slightly curved trunk with a natural taper from the base up. The first three branches proceed as in the formal upright with one difference – the bottom-most branch pulls in the direction opposite to the lean of the trunk. This balances the composition. At the crown, the leader bows slightly toward the viewer. The crown is so covered with foliage that the trunk is hidden from view, and in spite of the curve of the trunk, the crown should always sit directly above the base.

The *slanted* style is a tree with a single trunk with branches on both sides, but that exhibits a definite slant to one side or the other. Many such trees are seen in nature at the beach or on mountain cliffs where strong winds have "trained" the trunks and branches.

With formal upright, informal upright, and slanted styles, the number three is significant. The lowest branches are grouped in threes, and this grouping begins one-third of the way up the trunk. The bottom-most three branches almost encircle the trunk, with two branches thrusting forward, one slightly higher than the other. The third branch, emanating from a point between the first two, is set at such an angle as to make the foliage appear lower than the other two. This pattern presents an easy way to tell front from back, and sets the tone of the entire composition.

The growing tip of a *cascade* bonsai reaches below the base of the container. The trunk has a natural taper and gives the impression of the forces of nature pulling against the forces of gravity. Branches appear to be seeking the light. The winding main trunk is reminiscent of a stream meandering down the side of a mountain.

The tip of a *semicascade*, like the cascade, projects over the rim of the container, but does not drop below its base.

A beautiful slanting style bonsai from the Mansei-en Collection in Japan, this shows a definite lean to the left, although this is less pronounced than that found in many bonsai trained in this style – traditionally the trunk can make an angle of up to 45° from the vertical. The branches on the lower right of the trunk may have been wired to induce the downward slope, or perhaps have been hung with weights to pull the branch tips toward the ground. This example also shows another typical feature of slanted styles in that the roots to the right of the trunk, that is the opposite side from the direction of lean, have broken the soil surface, as if the buffeting wind responsible for the directional lean has come close to uprooting the tree at some time in the past. The rivets on the dark-brown earthenware container are traditional.

71

These are the five basic styles. Every other style is a development from, or a refinement of, one of these styles.

The *literati* bonsai, highly stylized and lyrical, is typified by a single long, graceful trunk supporting a minimum of branches which are usually clustered around the top.

A *coiled* bonsai has a trunk that is so convoluted it could almost encircle itself. It is a style rarely seen.

The *broom* is a very specific style. A single trunk resembling a straight, upside-down broom handle, culminates in finely ramified branches that form a fan-shape, almost like the fanned out bristles of an old-fashioned broom. The zelkova is the tree most frequently used to create this style.

A *split trunk* bonsai has a single trunk that is torn in two, with the trunk stripped bare of bark in the areas affected.

The *driftwood* style is a single trunk tree with a portion of dead trunk, bark, and/or branches. This dead wood appears bleached, like naturally created driftwood.

The *windswept* bonsai has all its branches leaning in a single direction, with the branches on one side of the trunk representing the effects of strong constant winds like those found beside the sea.

The *exposed root* style features bare stilt-like roots which, in effect, support the bonsai and grow out of the soil. The impression given is that the tree has endured years of severe weather.

The *root-over-rock* bonsai has exposed roots growing over and then down the sides of a rock. The roots survive in a thin margin of soil in the rock and are anchored in a larger amount in the container.

A *clinging-to-rock* bonsai has roots that are planted onto a rock and become attached to the rock itself.

The *twisted-trunk* is twisted either from natural causes or from a genetic trait inherent in the tree. In some cases the surrounding conditions could produce such growth, and it can be successfully reproduced artificially in bonsai.

LEFT: *Juniperus chinensis "Sargentii" Sargent juniper A dramatic example of the driftwood style, this literati-style bonsai is from the Mansei-en Collection. Some bonsaiists bleach the dead wood in their compositions – with wood furniture lightener or lime sulfur solution (see p. 81) – in order to get the characteristic weathered look and promote the esthetic contrast of light dead and strong brown or red-brown living wood.*

RIGHT: *Kyuzo Murata's nursery in Omiya. The forest planting benefits from the shade offered by the thatched roof and protection from wind afforded by the building, while those plantings on the ground are shaded by the low table on which the forest sits. Notice too that the whole area has been recently watered, to raise the humidity level.*

The *twin trunk* looks similar to a single trunk bonsai, divided in two at the baseline, but is, in fact, two trunks, one of which is taller and thicker than the other.

In a *clump* style bonsai, a cluster of close trunks grow from a single root.

The *stump* bonsai is a single root and a rounded "turtle back" trunk, from which several branches grow.

The *raft* is a single tree, laid on its side, with its branches trained upward to become individual trees, still connected by the single mother trunk.

The *sinuous* style features a single root which twists and turns under the soil, lending the grouping of trees rising from its trunk the look of individually rooted trees.

Multiple tree or *forest* groupings consist of three, five or more trees (sometimes more than twenty) in a single container. They represent a natural forest or grove of trees found in the wild. Below ten, even numbers are generally avoided, especially the number four.

Mixed plantings are a combination of grasses, herbs, and accompanying plants.

Saikei is a landscape, incorporating trees, shrubs, rocks, mosses, and lichens in any number or combination, and sometimes joined by natural elements like streams, waterfalls, sand, and water.

Tools for shaping

Most bonsai tools are still manufactured in Japan, although they are readily available in the West. They can be expensive, but if you are going to invest in tools, buying the best you can afford makes sense. It is sometimes possible to find sets of tools that are suitable for beginners, and which can work out cheaper than buying these tools individually. The disadvantage is that the selection has been made by someone else and may not suit the type of bonsai you choose to work with.

To begin with, you can probably use the basic tools that are already in your toolkit, and your general gardening tools, and postpone an investment in specialist bonsai tools until you are committed to the art. Initially, you will need:

- sharp pruning shears and a small, finely toothed saw for pruning thick stock
- fine, long-handled snips for trimming leaves and evergreens
- sharp, sterilized pruning knife
- pail(s) for mixing soil
- drainage material and potting soils
- blunt stick (a chopstick is ideal)
- stiff brush for smoothing soil surface
- pan large enough to soak bonsai when potted
- Lazy Susan (turntable) for turning plant
- nylon or plastic window screening
- scissors
- annealed copper wire strong enough to hold tree in pot and pot on table
- wire cutters
- watering can or hose with fine spray rosette
- dried/powdered/fresh moss/lichens/ground cover . . . your choice
- plant
- appropriate container
- small looseleaf notebook for recording date potted, wired, pruned, fed and dates it leafed out, flowered, fruited, coned, and so on.

Preshaping considerations

Juniperus chinensis "Sargentii"
Sargent juniper
This ninety-year-old slanting
style bonsai collected from the
mountains of Japan is a fine
example of living sculpture.
Sargent junipers often have a
driftwood appearance, which
adds to the aged look and
contrasts well with the red-brown
bark color. The earthtone
container, which is rectangular
and unglazed, also provides an
ideal complement to the bark.
This bonsai stands 34 inches
high, including the container.

Before you start to cut, you must know your tree and have a mental picture of its future shape. This does not have to be exact but it does have to be complete enough for you to decide what style the bonsai will ultimately assume.

Place your tree at eye level in such a way that you can view it from all directions without having to bend.

Developing a tree into a bonsai, from the initial evaluation on, is a logical process. First, place a small chalk mark on the trunk to record the starting point. This may seem unnecessary, but you can get lost in "thinking a tree", in other words, during the familiarization sessions with a new plant, and the chalk mark helps to define the starting point. Turn the tree 10° to the right again and again, until you have looked at the whole trunk and all the branches and the tree is back at its start.

To help in visualization during this period of exploration, the period about which, by the way, many bonsaiists have the most qualms, gently hold a small piece of plain brown paper in front of each branch in question. With the paper hiding the branch, it is much easier to tell how it enhances or detracts from the overall shape of the tree. In this way you can "see" how the pruned tree will look.

A plain backdrop helps, too. By simplifying the tree's surroundings, you can get an accurate picture of the tree without any visual competition. Readily available backdrops, like the side of the house or garage, or a piece of brown wrapping paper propped up along the back of your table, are all suitable.

Remember that every tree has a front, a back, and two sides, not just literally, but stylistically. You should always view from the front unless, of course, it is being worked on.

Determining the front and back of a tree is often obvious from the very nature of the plant material and the manner in which it is already growing. Sometimes, however, it is less than clear. Generally speaking, the front of a bonsai has a better taper to the trunk than the others and – if the trunk curves – the curves should be from side to side, not toward you. The front, too, shows the most pleasing arrangement of the branches, and the best view of the root structure. If you are unsure about which is the front of your tree, then look at it closely, think about it, look at full-size trees around you, and if necessary put it back in a holding bed until you "know" instinctively which side is its front, its back, indeed until you are sure about its whole style.

Naturally, with very young plants, the future offers many more options than with older, established trees. You will save considerable grief and wringing of hands over which branches to keep and which to remove, and over whether your subject will become a formal or informal upright if you choose to work with mature trees when possible, initially at least. If you use young saplings to create bonsai, you have to grow them to maturity in your mind's eye before you can start working on them.

It is worth remembering that bonsai take a long time to fulfil their artistic destinies. Some never do. Others do it admirably. Since the art of bonsai is difficult for a basically impatient soul to practice, opt for a head start. Try creating a few bonsai from older plants. Dig some up from the overgrown, often neglected foundation plantings around your home and around those of friends and relatives. Get their permission first and replace them with appropriate plants that will probably be more in scale with the house anyway. To the confirmed bonsaiist, nothing is sacred — everything is a potential bonsai.

It also helps to work on inexpensive or free, even inappropriate, material at first, just to practice and gain some experience at pruning. In that way you won't be hurting anything of real or potential value and you can work with more freedom.

How to cut

A concave cut heals more quickly than any other. When pruning primary branches, make the cut with a pair of concave Japanese pruners. If you do not have these, make a flat cut, afterward digging into the bark with a very sharp pruning knife so that the edges of the wound are level with the plane of the trunk. Treat secondary branches in the same manner.

When shortening a branch, plan a diagonal cut with the longest remaining edge on the upper plane just above a node. In this way, the scars will heal faster and be less noticeable, if they are noticeable at all.

The best way to deal with a large branch is to remove it with a saw or a special Japanese clipper called a *kuikiri* trimmer. With a saw, first make a shallow cut under the branch as close to the trunk or the place where the branch is to end as you can. Then saw through the rest of the branch from the top. If the branch does not come free when both the upper and lower cuts are made and meet, give it a gentle tug. It will separate itself from the main branch or trunk with no harm to the rest of the tree. If you have a *kuikiri* trimmer, grasp the branch with the trimmer, then twist the

How to make a cut

1 *After branch pruning, a dead stump often has to be removed. Use curved branch cutters, available in a variety of sizes, if possible.*

2 *You can apply a flexible healing compound to the cut to spur healing, but the wound will heal perfectly well without this treatment.*

3 *A concave cut heals flat, the cambium forming a callus. A flat cut, on the other hand, would heal with an unsightly bump.*

trimmer until the bark is cut and the wood is penetrated, then completely severed.

In each case, if a sizeable scar remains, carve the scar with a sharp pruning knife so it comes to a taper at one or both ends, if possible, then smooth any remaining rough spots. This will help the healing process. If the scar is very large, recess its edges and then, with the pruning knife, carve the center of the wound into a pointed, almost pyramidal, shape. As the wound heals, a callus will grow toward the point and will leave a smooth, flat surface in its wake.

Pruning

Pruning is at the very center of the art of bonsai. Without it, very few examples of plants would have developed into viable bonsai.

Can a look of age, grace, stability, and character be achieved with pruning alone? The answer has to be yes, but it would take far more time and skill and patience than most people have. So, the majority of bonsaiists use ancillary techniques to help them achieve their goals. These are traditional methods, employed to correct, reposition, encourage, or discourage growth. They are based on long experience in bringing out all there is to bring out in a tree, and many of them can be grouped under the general heading of pruning.

Major pruning of any kind should be reserved for the period of the tree's strongest growth, when it has the power to recover and generate fine branching. If this branching is pruned in turn, it produces even finer branching. In this way, over a period of time, the tree is guided into a shape that is appropriate for a mature specimen of the species, one which is in proportion with the trunk and in which branching, leaf growth, flowering, and berrying are all present, at an appropriate size.

There are two basic methods of pruning: one used primarily for shaping fruiting and flowering subjects, and one for all other plants. Flowering and fruiting trees generally flower and fruit on the previous year's growth. New shoots, therefore, should be removed near the base of the branch, leaving one or two buds so that blossoms are guaranteed for the next season. If all the new shoots were allowed to grow unchecked, the plant's energy would go into the growing tips, rather than the new buds and shoots. As a result, the new tip growth would thicken and elongate with little – if any – ramification, while the new buds and new growth thin and weaken.

Bud pinching

1 *On deciduous plants, pinch out any new buds that, if left to grow unchecked, would detract from the overall design.*

2 *New growth on needled plants, such as this juniper, should never be cut. Identify the overgrown shoot and hold it with one hand.*

3 *Pull the overgrown shoot away with the fingers of your other hand. This encourages needle production.*

Pruning by bud pinching keeps new buds from taking over and contributes to sending nutrients and energy to the fledgling buds farther back on the branch. This, in turn, creates thicker, healthier growth. Bud pinching also encourages ramification, which maintains branchlets in sufficient numbers and fine enough to produce a bonsai in proper scale and proportion, while lessening the amount of nutrition needed to feed the tree. As a result, the tree is physically "open" to both good air circulation and light. In other words, bud pinching is needed to improve the overall configuration of the tree, to contribute to the development of woody and leafy parts, and to encourage cone and fruit production.

Lush needle production is encouraged by pinching the tip growth. A portion of the new bud (or new candle) on both the longer branches and some of the shorter branches should be twisted free from the parent. This is done by firmly but gently grasping the developing candle between two fingers of one hand and twisting off between half and a third of the candle tip. By doing this, you will prevent excessive elongation of the branch, which will also help to thicken the needle masses on the rest of the branch.

Candle pruning encourages rapid thickening and eliminates the need to prune with clippers, which always leaves a scar. In many popular varieties of trees, new shoots are in constant production throughout the year. These shoots must be pinched as soon as they appear.

With deciduous trees, too, new growth should be pinched off and only the one or two buds closest to the base of the branch or trunk saved. This again will result in fine twig development or ramification.

At all times any poorly located buds that spontaneously emerge on the trunk and main branches should be removed. The exception to this is if one or more of them will eventually fill in a sparse area or develop into a branch where a branch is needed. In that case, the new bud should be retained and developed.

Naturally, there are some precautions to take. First, bud pinching should be postponed on newly pruned and potted trees until they have regained their strength. Also, bud pinching must be done at the proper time, in the proper way, which can vary from tree to tree.

When a new shoot is dramatically reduced, its new growth forms a right angle with the old growth, thereby giving the branch a new direction. When, the following year, the tip is pruned, the new growth will again be in the opposite direction. The branch will soon become a tracery of right and left turns, which will "open up" the tree and

How to prune

1 *On evergreens, wait until the shoot has hardened off, and cut where a new shoot is growing. This makes the cut difficult to see.*

2 *This tree obviously needs pruning. Using long-handled snippers, cut to a shoot that is growing in the direction you want.*

3 *After pruning, the tree's basic shape is again visible. This is the method to follow for deciduous trees.*

allow the development of a thick, gnarled look, typical of old trees. In addition, much of the trunk and branching configuration, which creates a look of age, grace, and stability will be visible, which is as it should be.

Major shaping

Major, even drastic, pruning is frequently needed when a tree is about to begin its life as a bonsai, when – if it does not already have one – it must be given a direction for growth.

Some people think of shaping tactics as cruel and unnatural. On the contrary, they actually help the tree to become its best possible self, without allowing the sometimes disastrous accidents of fate to take their toll. It is a fact that most bonsai are a good deal healthier than those trees left to chance.

It is important to remember that pruning any portion of a tree encourages new healthy growth in that same area. Thus root pruning will encourage new root growth, and top pruning will encourage new top growth.

When you look at a tree in nature first its trunk and then its branches create the greatest impression. The trunk and the branches are also the tree's largest physical features, all of which can tend to intimidate the beginner. Your best course is to practice on inexpensive or free material. In choosing something suitable, look for a trunk that has greater girth at the base than at the top and exhibits a decided taper as it reaches its apex. Depending on the style most appropriate to your material, eliminate branches that detract from the ultimate design. Study photographs and illustrations of trees trained in that style. Then plan the course your tree will take.

No matter what the style, every tree has a "leader". Even if your tree has two leaders, as in the case of a twin trunk, one will be sturdier and taller than the other. If you are not working with a twin trunk, you may choose to eliminate one. However, if there are two or three trunks which do not relate to each other gracefully, you may want to eliminate some or all but the main trunk.

Once the main trunk is established, turn your attention to the branching of the tree. First, eliminate branches that are dead, unless they might play an important part in the eventual design. Next, cut out any overly long or crossing branches that grow into the heart of the tree, or that mar its shape. Cut the limbs off at their bases, as close to the trunk as possible. If the branch is a very healthy one which you feel might be inclined to sprout, leave a small portion on the tree, and gradually reduce its size over the season. In this way, sprouting will be prevented.

Contrary to common belief, the dormant season is a busy one for the bonsaiist since that is the time much of the pruning can be done, with no harm to the tree. Choose a day that is not bitterly cold. Completely eliminate any stubs you have previously preserved at the base of growing branches and prune out any unnecessary branches in dense, well-branched areas.

This is a critically important time in the styling of flowering and fruiting material. Study the tree carefully to insure that flowering will be evenly distributed, and that the quantity of flowers on any given branch will not visually overpower the other branches.

Deciduous trees can survive drastic reapportioning, even at a mature age, which is something that full-grown evergreens cannot do. The major pruning of evergreens should take place when they are young and supple, with supplementary training carried out by wiring (see pp. 82–5), bud pinching, and trimming.

When pruning an evergreen branch, remove the growth from in front of the node to the tip of the branch – be sure to leave the node on the tree. As with any drastically pruned tree, however, the stump of the branch removed should be cut flush with the trunk. If necessary, use a sharp pruning knife for the finishing touches.

You can encourage a new branch to grow in a barren area by reducing the other branches on the tree. Watch carefully for the telltale swelling of buds. As they swell, decide which node could produce a branch in the proper position, and as the other buds begin to grow, eliminate them, allowing all the plant's energy to concentrate on the one remaining sprout.

There are some precautions you can take to increase your chances of success. Before you prune any tree, be certain that it is in good health, unless you plan to eliminate only dead or diseased growth. Pruning is a stressful process and only healthy plants have the energy to heal the resulting wounds.

Naturally, it is advisable to select material that demands the least amount of training to become admirable representatives of the art of bonsai, but that is not always possible or affordable. More likely, at some time, you will find yourself faced with a plant that presents a challenge. Its trunk, branches or root may have a major flaw. Don't despair: work with the tree if you like it. With proper pruning, wiring, and accommodation, you could overcome its faults.

It may be obvious but it bears repeating that the object of shaping and pruning is to help a tree become a prime specimen of its kind, embodying the best natural characteristics of the mature tree. Your constant inspiration should be the species itself, and your goal is to create that ideal in miniature.

The jin

Often in nature the unexpected happens. A tree is struck by lightning, or it falls, taking with it a branch or leader from a neighboring tree. Or a branch suddenly, and for no apparent reason, withers and dies, leaving a woody, sometimes gnarled branch of dead wood behind. This in bonsai is called a jin.

As part of nature's action, it is accepted as part of life. For that reason, bonsaiists have learned how to recreate this phenomenon artificially.

Before you start to create a jin, you have to decide whether or not, artistically, the tree is a good candidate for a jin; horticulturally, if it is an appropriate candidate for a jin; and, technically, if you feel able to create a jin. The single condition under which most jins are created is when an appropriate tree must undergo drastic pruning, usually either to reduce its height, or to reduce the length of an important branch.

The tools you need for this process are: snippers to loosen and strip off bark, and to remove the tips of branches in order to bare an area to start the jin; pruning shears or saw to cut the branch that will become the jin; and pliers to grasp and tear the limb. (Special jinning pliers are available, but ordinary ones are adequate for beginners.)

The most appropriate trees for jins are the evergreens, such as junipers, yews, firs, pines, spruces, and cedars. The limbs of most conifers, when trimmed of all needles on a branch, will die of their own volition, and the bark will peel naturally. Deciduous trees, except for oaks, are rarely used as subjects for a jin.

Start with the leader. Turn the tree around so the back faces you. Cut halfway through the leader and, grasping the partially severed tip, bend it in the opposite direction until it breaks – you will hear a snapping sound. Then turn the tree around. The partially severed tip plus some bark or fiber will probably still be clinging to the trunk. Grasp the tip firmly, pull downward and tear the entire piece from the trunk, severing the connection.

This downward tug will also pull additional bark and fiber from the bonsai. This is as it should be because, with this jagged, informal configuration, the tree will look as though nature, not man, was responsible for the tear.

On top, the cut that began the process will be jarringly obvious, and it will not look in the least natural. Your task now is to reduce the evidence of manipulation by snipping, grasping, and pulling off little sections of the flat incision.

With shears, snip a tiny vertical slot down through the flat surface of the incision. Then grasp the resulting bit of wood with your pliers, pulling it downward in a straight

---

How to jin a branch

1 *The top of this* Pinus parviflora *(Japanese white pine) has died because training wire was left on too long. Instead of removing it, it can be cut and bleached to form a jin. Cut off any wood you don't want with branch cutters.*

2 *Remove the bark and cambium layer from the remaining branch with a sharp, sterilized knife. The jin gives an immediate look of age to the tree.*

line. Ideally, it should be pulled down to a live branch, where the cambium layer (that is, the layer between wood and bark) and bark hold fast. Continue to snip sections of the top, to both the right and left of the center of the emerging jin, rolling them downward with the pliers, and allowing them to separate from the tree.

As you peel, always follow the natural course of the wood grain so that the live material to the right and left of the peel is undamaged. Throughout the peeling process, be sure to remove both the cambium layer and the inner layer of bark to expose the core wood.

Little by little the flat cut on top will become smaller and more pointed. Eventually, by steadily repeating the process, you will have created a tapered point. At this time, you have a choice. You can either end the peeling process as you near the next live branch, or you can continue the process downward, even to the base of the trunk and out onto a root. You are the one who must decide.

If, however, you are creating a jin from a branch rather than a leader, the branch should be bare and look completely dead. To make the jin look more natural, where the branch meets the trunk, remove a small amount of bark to indicate the struggle that the tree waged in trying to preserve its limb.

When you are satisfied that you have removed enough bark, and that an appropriate amount of dead wood is showing, clean up round the trunk or branch with a wire brush to remove any last pieces of cambium. Electric rotating wire brushes are available from bonsai nurseries, but you can use a hand one of a suitable size and texture, if you prefer.

During the summer, it is a good idea to treat the jin with lime sulfur to ward off potential rot. Choose a hot, sunny day when the leaves and wood of the tree are completely dry. Cover the rest of the tree, including branches, trunk, roots and soil, with something waterproof like thin plastic, aluminum foil, or water-repellent fabric. Add just enough water to a small amount of powdered lime sulfur to make a thick paste. With a small, pointed artist's brush, paint the jin with the paste, trying not to drop any on neighboring live plant. Immediately after its application, the paste will produce a white blush on the wood, which will fade and eventually disappear, leaving only the natural look of the wood itself.

For the most effective results, repeat this process twice during the hottest parts of the summer, once at the beginning and once at the end, two years in a row, and then whenever you think there is a danger of rot setting in.

OPPOSITE: Juniperus rigida
Needle juniper
This clump-style needle juniper is from the Mansei-en Collection in Japan. The artistic dead wood weaves round the two main trunks, and jins have been created from several of the shorter branches. The short, sharply pointed, bright-green needles and red-brown bark contrast well with the driftwood effect. Needle junipers are evergreen, their foliage turning an attractive green-bronze in winter.

The look of age

There are various elements that make us believe that a tree is old. In order for you to be able to create the illusion of age in plants that are young, you have to know what those elements are.

If you could look at a forest tree with which nature had had its way, with which man and progress and municipal pruning had not trifled, you would observe several characteristics rarely seen any more.

The branches on the lower quarter of the trunk might be dead or missing because of intense shade; the branches might have grown shorter as they proceed up the trunk, with the shortest growing closest to the crown; the tree, especially if it was an evergreen, would culminate in a thick mass of needles or leaves at the top; scars might dapple the trunk where deer or falling trees had scraped the bark; cones or berries might decorate the branches; and surface roots might protrude far above ground level. Perhaps most important, a big, thick trunk that tapered upward, holding all those branches, cones, fruits, and even birds' nests, through years of storms, wind, and temperature fluctuations, would support this whole mini-ecosystem.

The trunk is what the bonsaiist tries to emulate in creating trees that appear mature, yet in chronological terms may not be. Pruning is of prime importance in this process. Repeated trimming in the formative years develops trees that exhibit some or all of the traits of age, and that assume a look that the young seedling, left in the garden to grow in its own way, in its own time, may never exhibit simply because civilization and acts of nature may not allow it to.

One of the time-honored techniques used to bring out those characteristics is the repeated cutting back of top growth. As the process is repeated, the trunk will slowly thicken, developing bulges and crags. It will also acquire a taper as some of the new buds are removed and you choose a different, slimmer leader to train upright.

To do this, wiring is used. Repeating this process, each time reducing the remaining leader, will help you to create the necessary taper, adding a feeling of age that would not ordinarily exist in such a short time.

Young and old plants are dealt with in different ways. Young material should be encouraged to grow all its branches as long as it is appropriate for the tree and its long-term design. After the season's new growth is in, it should be evaluated, then pruned. With old material, pruning growth early will exaggerate the stunting effect.

One method used effectively to thicken the trunks of new and even old material is to plant it directly in a development bed for a period of months, sometimes years. During that time, it is treated as a bonsai in almost every respect. It is root pruned and top pruned at the proper time, and watered and fed. It can also be root pruned to prevent the growth of tap roots and encourage the growth of fine feeder roots. In many instances, trees that begin to deviate from the grand scheme envisaged for them can be wired. In fact, everything is done for the tree that would be done for a potted bonsai with one exception: all the bottom branches are left on the tree. The more low branches there are on the tree, the more top and leaf growth there will be. And the more top and leaf growth there is, the thicker the trunk will be to support it all, which certainly adds to the look of age.

That look is also enhanced by creating a jin. If the conditions that lend themselves to making a jin of the leader don't exist, some bonsaiists tear a primary branch that emanates from the trunk, removing most of the bark and leaving in its wake a jagged stump evocative of weathering, accidents, or lightning.

Wiring and branch hanging

There are three reasons for wiring bonsai-in-training. The first is to set the bonsai into the shape it is to hold when the wires are finally removed. The second is to hold the bonsai tree in its pot. The less mentioned third is to anchor the bonsai pot to its stand.

Wiring for shape
When wiring for shape you are attempting to manipulate the plant so that it assumes the position you have decided is ideal for that tree. It involves trunk, roots, branches, branchlets – literally every growing portion of the tree. With pruning, wiring is the most common method of inducing a new shape. It is also used to maintain shape, in that branchlets whose unchecked growth might alter the shape you have chosen are also wired.

A tree should be fed weeks before wiring takes place and it should be well watered immediately after wiring.

No matter what the extent of the wiring, the techniques employed are the same. First, you should make a visual evaluation of the tree, trying to understand its needs and its growth habits. Then, sketch out the ultimate shape you are aiming for, and evaluate it further. Only then should you begin actual wiring.

Wiring a tree

1 *Start by securing the wire into the rootball, then wrap the wire round the trunk. Try to keep the wire at a 45° angle to the trunk.*

2 *When wiring branches, wire two together, so that one exerts pressure on the other. The thinner the branch, the finer the wire to use.*

3 *The tree loses its shrubby look once the wire is in place. Be sure to remove wires before they start to "bite" into the trunk or branches.*

Annealed copper wire is used for wiring bonsai. Since the wire will be bent around the plant in a kind of outer sculptural form, it must at the same time be easy to bend yet firm enough to hold its shape. Grades of copper wire are available according to thickness. Number 2, the thickest usually necessary, is strong enough to bend a 3 inch tree trunk, depending on the tree, and hold it in position. If you find that more tensile strength is necessary, add a second wire of the same thickness alongside the first. Number 24, one of the finest, is perfect for wiring fragile branch tips. The numbers in between, graduating from 4 to 22, are used for all the various jobs in between.

If you purchase your wire at a bonsai nursery, it will probably be annealed, but check first. If, however, you buy it in a hardware or DIY store, it will almost certainly not be annealed and you will have to do it yourself. Place the wire, either in straight lengths or in coils, on a gas or electric stove's heating element, or on an outdoor barbeque, over a low heat. As the copper heats, it will gradually change from a bright copper color to a cherry red when finished. The thicker the wire, the longer it will take to anneal. As it cools, it will tone down to a dull red. Allow it to cool and store it in a cool place, either in the same shape it was when annealed, or coiled loosely around a small log.

Before beginning the wiring process, bend the trunk or branch gently several times in the direction of its future shape. If the wood is too inflexible to allow this, some bonsaiists make a very shallow cut on the trunk or branch where the bend is to be created before the wire is applied. This is not usually necessary, however. It is easiest to uncoil wire from a spool. Since it is already slightly looped, it is easier to judge the length needed for the job at hand. If a branch of medium thickness measures approximately 12 inches in length, add about another 9–12 inches to insure proper coverage for the branch. When in doubt, double the length of the wire. Then, with wire, wire cutters, floral tape to paper the wire, pruning shears, a few small rubber patches, hemp string, a jack or lever, and the plant to be wired to hand, begin by removing the dead or unwanted portions of the plants.

How to wire
When you have eliminated all the material you do not want, anchor the wire by inserting it into the soil as deeply as possible behind, and at a 45° angle to, the trunk. Then twist the wire in a diagonal spiral around the trunk, to the right if the bend will be to the right, or to the left if the bend will be to the left. Loop it around in sufficiently loose coils so that

the wire will not dig into the bark and make permanent indentations, but not so loose that it will move up and down. If the bark is soft or weak due either to its condition or to the species of tree itself, or if you have any doubts about the bark's ability to stand up to contact with wire, wrap the wire first in floral tape.

Now start wiring, beginning at the bottom of the trunk and proceeding up to the lowest branch, then the next-to-lowest branch and so on up the tree as far as the wiring is to go. Always begin wiring from the bottom, since this is the only way to insure the proper placement of branches and the proper skew of the trunk.

Hold the inserted end of the wire and the plant in one hand while coiling the wire around the plant, between buds, leaves, and nodes, with the other. Afterward, correct the angle of the limb by slowly rotating it in the direction in which the wire runs or by placing both your thumbs on the inside line of the bend and pushing outward.

If you only want to wire one branch, coil the end of the wire around the trunk or trunk wire several times from above the branch in question, then run it out onto the branch. Allow a bit of copper to protrude beyond the tip of the branch you are wiring and bend it down and behind the branch tip. This will give you a handle to help remove the wire when removal time comes. (If you are removing very thick wire, the best procedure is to cut it off in small pieces.)

There are times when two branches can be trained with one long wire – one branch will exert the necessary leverage on the other. Begin at the junction of the branches, bending the wire into a hairpin shape. Loop the wire around the junction, then twist one side of the "hairpin" several times around the lower branch. Loop the free end of the wire a few times around the upper branch. At this point, when both branches are started, you can go back and complete the wiring of the lower branch and then the upper branch. Both branches will be held fast.

It is more difficult to correct the shape of a thickened trunk. First wrap the trunk with garden twine to protect it from indentations. Place thick copper wire straight up the trunk following the grain, then immediately wrap a slender wire around the trunk. This will help keep the original wires together so their bending action will work in tandem with each other, resulting in twice the strength. Then proceed as usual, twisting gently in the direction of the coil and the ultimate direction of the bend.

It depends on their thickness, of course, but most tree trunks will take shape within a year, branches may take only four or five months, and branchlets only two to three

months. Keep newly wired material in a shady, protected area for several days, since its ability to withstand sun and wind has been temporarily reduced. If it is in leaf or needle, mist daily to reduce the strain on its root system. Do not wire weak or newly transplanted trees for a year or more, depending on their energy level.

Using jacks and levers

When a trunk is too thick to respond to wiring, a jack or lever can be used. Both these methods involve wrapping the trunk first with twine for protection.

When using a jack, wrap the trunk, and make several strands of the string at each end 1 inch or so longer than the others, so that the ends of the jack can be slipped under them – they will both hold the jack in place, and protect the trunk. Hook the longer strands onto the ends of the jack, and place a rubber pad against the trunk where the screw will be tightened against the trunk. Then gently maneuver the screw against the trunk, creating a bend. As time passes, the jack should be tightened until the trunk is positioned where you think it should be.

When using a lever to bend a trunk, you have to create a sling-shot configuration. Tie rope or heavy string to both sides of the section of trunk to be changed. With the lever, exert pressure into the sling and away from the trunk, thereby creating a bend. Generally, however, these two techniques are reserved for the drastic changing of mature, thick material only.

When to wire

With deciduous plants for instance, it is easier to see the architecture and easier to wire without foliage. Many plants are wired in winter for a variety of reasons. If the plant is ensconced in a developing bed or cold-frame, venture out during a mild period and bring it inside and wire in the warmth of the house – this will help warm the plant tissues so that the branches are more flexible and more easily worked. Place the tree back in the bed or cold-frame when you have finished to continue its overwintering.

There are general guidelines about the timeliness of wiring for specific varieties. First, it is easiest to wire willow, juniper, pine, and the like because they are the most flexible species and adapt quickly to training. Conifers, despite their flexibility, are the toughest category to induce to maintain a new shape. They can take as long as a year to train in the desired manner and then may still revert to their original form. The best time to wire conifers tends to be in late fall or early winter.

Deciduous plants, like azaleas and maples, are most tractable in late spring or early summer, after buds have developed and leaves have unfurled but before the new growth has hardened. They grow so quickly, however, that you must keep a careful eye on them since their tender new growth could easily be strangled by its frame of copper. These trees take training very well, settling into their new shapes within a matter of months.

One of the last things to do in fall, just before you put the trees in the winter storage area, is to remove the wires put on the year before. This is because some trees could be injured from coils that tighten around their fast-growing shoots.

Branch hanging

Lead weights used for weighting fishing lines, and those for drapes, can also be used for training branches. Attach the weights, available in fishing tackle stores or departments stores, to light nylon fishing line (this is colorless, strong and inexpensive), tie the line to the middle or tip of the branch, depending on its natural configuration, and allow the hanging weight to pull the branch down to the appropriate point. Should the angle or curve not be to your liking or the shape of the branch unnatural, you can correct it by anchoring the weight to either the trunk, another branch, or to a copper wire that spans the top of the container.

Always make sure that the fishing line is not cutting into the bark of the branch. If it does begin to do so, insert a small piece of rubber padding under the loop to prevent scarring.

Anchoring bonsai

It takes only a moment to provide a secure anchorage for the bonsai both in its pot and on its display table. When potting the bonsai, run a few loops of wire through the drainage holes in the bottom of the container (see pp. 89–90), and up over the rootball or the main roots at the base of the trunk. Protect the roots with a small piece of rubber where the copper comes in contact with them.

When both ends of the wire are protruding, tie them together or twist them firmly around a slender but strong piece of wood or metal, thereby binding the two together. Also, run a few wires over the surface of the pot and around the top of its display table so that the pot is securely anchored onto its shelf.

Pinus parviflora
Japanese white pine
A cascade style bonsai from the Oguchi Collection, Japan, in which the tip of the trunk does indeed fall below the base of the container, in this case a round unglazed brown earthenware pot with an outward-curving lip. The trunk shows great strength and age, and gives a clear impression of having been buffeted by strong winds and, perhaps, of having endured heavy snowfalls. Wiring, which is still visible on some of the branches, has been used to accentuate their horizontal spread. The moss and other ground cover plants also contribute to the aged appearance of this bonsai.

Leaf pruning

In choosing plants for training into bonsai, it is preferable that ones with attributes suited to the future appearance of the species be chosen. Among the most important concern leaf size; plants with small leaves will be in scale when depicted as a tree much reduced in size whereas ones with disproportionately large leaves will appear incongruous. Unfortunately, it is not always possible to select only small-leaved plants. All too often, plants with promising form and proportion, but with leaves larger than desirable, become available and it is with these subjects that leaf pruning can be resorted to to reduce the size of the leaves.

In leaf pruning, part or all of a leaf is removed. The rationale for this practice is to encourage the growth of a new set of leaves from the bud at the base of the petiole or leaf stalk. These leaves will usually be smaller and more in keeping with the scale and overall size of the dwarfed tree. In some species, the shape of the leaves, especially the better defined indentations along the leaf edges, where applicable, is of desirable esthetic value.

There are two main ways to leaf prune. One is to remove the entire leaf blade and its stalk. This method also encourages the sprouting of the bud in the leaf axil so contributing to a fuller top growth. The other method is to remove a part of the leaf blade or the whole leaf blade with just the petiole remaining. While this method avoids damaging the dormant bud between the petiole and shoot, the presence of the petiole or even part of it may inhibit the sprouting of the bud. Sprouting will more likely occur when the petiole is shed some two or more weeks after pruning.

Trees scheduled for leaf pruning ought to be in a healthy condition. They should be prepared ahead of time by being fed regularly, preferably with dilute manure tea (see p.57), for a season or at least a month or two beforehand.

Leaves should not be pruned every year unless the tree is young and exceptionally vigorous. It is wise to allow for a year's recovery and restoration to optimum health after a rigorous regime of thinning or pruning of foliage. This is especially the case where, as sometimes practiced in Japan, all or most of the leaves are removed in the early summer from plants such as maples and zelkovas. Some or all terminal buds may also be removed to induce side buds to grow and produce a new or second flush of leaves.

After pruning, keep the bonsai in a semi-shaded spot until the new leaves appear. Full sun will stress the tree unnecessarily and deep shade may not provide enough light for food production due to leaves having been reduced in number. Remember too that while awaiting the emergence of new leaves, overwatering is to be avoided; with reduced leaves, the tree will not require as much water as usual.

Leaf pruning is more than a technique to scale down the size of the leaves. The removal of all or some of a tree's leaves can accomplish several important things: it can open up a tree to emphasize the beautiful form of its branching or its general shape. With the growth of new leaves, the chances of a higher-than-usual number of buds being induced to grow out can increase the branching (ramification) so enchancing the tree-like effect. The goal can also be cosmetic, ridding the tree of damaged, discolored or diseased leaves or for shaping by reducing the number of leaves in a section that appears top-heavy.

The pruning of leaves is generally done in early to mid-summer. If done too early when the sap is flowing strongly, new leaves will be produced in abundance and will often be larger than the original; if done later, fewer buds will sprout and this will result in fewer leaves being produced.

Trees that respond well to the pruning of leaves include most of the deciduous trees, including zelkovas, trident and Japanese maples, elms and birches. Beeches should have only out-of-scale leaves pinched out, allowing the other still immature leaves to develop, usually into a smaller size. Trees that should not be leaf pruned or pruned with caution are the conifers as well as the deciduous and evergreen trees that do not branch readily, such as Ginkgo and hornbeam.

The technique used on needled trees like podocarpus and five-needled pine is different from that used on deciduous material, and again is only appropriate for young, healthy trees. In addition, if the bonsai has been in training for a few years, despite its youth and health, you should not attempt this method. In fact, the only podocarpus and five-needled pines that should experience this treatment are those specimens that have overly long, bushy or curled needles. These should be pruned, leaving only about 1 inch of needle in their place. The next spring the needles that emerge will be shorter, automatically reducing the length of future needles, allowing smaller inside branches to get more sun and grow more buds.

Pines are frequently subjected to needle pulling if they are young and healthy. It is preferable to cut the needles completely at the base, taking care not to damage the bark or small twigs. This treatment can be done at any time of year unless the needles are too young and tender.

With junipers, cypress, and other trees with scale-like leaves, avoid needle pulling (unless the tree is very bushy) with excessively long needles; if it is it should be clipped.

Leaf pruning

Leaf pruning should be done when the tree is in an active growth spurt.
Cut off all the leaves, leaving the petioles, which will drop off naturally.
New leaves should grow within a few weeks.

Trees that are not suitable candidates for this treatment include yew, cedar, and spruce.

Root pruning

Every tree has roots and all root systems have a shape. Some are one sided, others are full; some have long tap roots, while others have a full set of fine feeder roots; some have surface roots with interesting shapes and bark, and others not, and so on.

Whatever shape roots may take, their health is of prime importance. The initiated bonsaiist looks up and looks down: looks at the top growth and looks at the root system. Before taking a blade to a root, it is important to understand that the tree is only as good as its root system. This is the funnel through which all nutrients are accessed and then distributed. By looking at the top growth of a tree, either in nature or in a bonsai pot, you will know a lot about its root system. If the branches have good extension, so does the root system. If all parts of the tree seem nourished and healthy, then it is probable that the root system is in good health. If any portion of the upper growth is less than good, the root system may well be to blame.

Root pruning is a regular occurrence in the life of a bonsai, since it not only helps that more fibrous root system

to emerge but, as an added bonus, maintains a plant that is healthy enough to accept top pruning and training while living in a small container.

Root pruning generally begins when a new tree joins a collection. It undergoes extra scrutiny, then pruning, when it is about to graduate from a plant-in-training to a bonsai. It will experience root pruning repeatedly: during repotting; during soil revitalization; and during the pruning of top growth when it has been altered sufficiently to warrant a simultaneous pruning of the growth below. As it is done, the development of a healthy, full root system, as well as the miniaturization of the plant, is furthered.

To begin with, the roots of freshly dug or newly purchased nursery-grown plants should be carefully inspected. If the tree has an interesting bark that might be damaged during this process, protect it by wrapping the area of trunk you will be holding with a strip of crêpe bandage or a folded cloth. Remove the plant from its bed of soil, container, or burlap wrapping, and if possible place it on a surface that rotates. An ordinary revolving spice rack set up on a few bricks or a stack of books or boards will do as long as it is sturdy and does not tip or wobble. As soon as you bare the roots, they begin to dry. The longer a root is exposed to the air, the more likely it is to suffer from drying. Since time is such a critical element now, the object is to work quickly and, when necessary, to mist the roots to keep them lightly moist, not sopping wet.

Trace a chalk mark about one-third of the way out from the base of the tree trunk toward the rim of the container, in a circle around the tree, to denote the extent of the new rootball to be kept intact. This also represents the surface area of the new pot, which means that, theoretically, the pot should be three times the size of the circle. The remaining two-thirds of the soil should be removed, starting at the surface and moving down. Poke a chopstick, or other blunt stick, into the rootball and wiggle it back and forth to loosen, then dislodge, the soil. This helps to prevent any root damage.

At this point, the tree plus one-third of its original soil and all of its roots are on the turntable ready for the next step. Lift the plant into the air. From the front, with the roots hanging down, cut those roots that grow out sideways by about one-third, and the bottom ones as short as possible, leaving about 1–3 inches of root material (root length can be altered depending on the depth of the chosen container). Mentally divide the remaining ball of soil into pie slices, depending on the size of the ball, probably

A stump bonsai from the Ueda Collection in Japan, this tree is remarkable for its sturdy trunk whose thick base and gnarled "turtle back" give an impression of great age. The arrangement of the branches, too, contributes to this feeling: a single branch at the base, as if the tree has lost the rest over time (there are areas on the trunk where the outer layer of bark has been removed as the branches were torn off), with all the others right at the top of the trunk, struggling to reach out for the light. Fine ramification, with no crossing branches, dense foliage, groundcover plants, and a complementary container also contribute to its success.

between six and twelve. Then, with a sterilized knife, carefully cut out every other slice until you have encircled the tree. Soil and roots will fall away from the tree, leaving the tree with some of its old soil to which new soil, to encourage new root growth, will be added.

Be sure to retain as many fine roots as possible, since they will provide the nourishment for the plant while new roots are being generated. If you find that the root configuration is imbalanced, developed on only two or three sides, for example, make an incision with the knife where you think

roots should be growing. Then plant the tree in either a bed of sand or a sand-filled container. New roots will start to grow within a matter of months.

Old or decayed roots, as well as tap roots, make it difficult to pot the tree and impede young, healthy growth. They must be removed. By doing this, you will encourage the active growth of fine feeding roots throughout the rootball. This, in turn, will help to preserve a balanced supply of water for the tree and establish a mechanism for anchoring the tree in its future container. Logically, the roots should always be pruned with a horizontal bottom plane. This creates an easy and level seat for the bonsai when it is placed in its pot.

Pruning a heavy tap root may have to span a period of years, which will mean that you must use a deeper container at first. It could mean that the tree should be placed back in a development bed for a season. Generally, however, the tap root should be taken back as far as it can go to allow easy placement of the plant in its container.

Remember that when you remove a significant number of roots, you must also remove a proportion of top growth, so that the remaining root mass will support the tree. Generally, young plants can stand the loss of up to two-thirds of their roots, older specimens only one-third.

The following season, deficient or underdeveloped roots should be removed and viable ones pruned again slightly to encourage still further branching.

Root pruning is best viewed as a method of keeping a plant healthy rather than a way of keeping it small. Its response to a slight pruning of the root mass might be to produce even more twig growth and leaves than expected. This is normal and can be kept under control with top pruning. Sometimes, however, the tree can go into shock, particularly after a drastic root pruning. That is the time to return the tree to a development bed, keep a constant watch on it and give it extra care and time – it could take as long as a year to work through the effects of root pruning.

Potting

Potting is an exacting process in that there are specific steps to take from start to finish. These steps, however, are not filled with mystery and will help you in potting house and greenhouse plants as well.

To begin, set up a work place in the shade and protected from the wind. This is necessary for several reasons. The plant is soon to go through a stressful procedure. It will be taken from its container, denuded of most of its soil, root pruned, top pruned, possibly wired, and then set into a new container. If, in addition, the tree must also deal with hot sunlight and drying winds, its ability to cope will be considerably reduced.

Preparing the container

Since horticultural concerns far outweigh others, prepare the container before touching the plant. The container you choose should ideally be shallow and fairly wide. The average bonsai pot is about one and a half times as large as the bonsai it contains, although with very dwarf or low, spreading trees it may be nearly one-third again as large. Unglazed training pots are best for young plants, since they are porous and therefore promote good aeration and root growth.

Cut a piece of screening to fit over the drainage holes. This serves two main purposes: it prevents soil particles from washing out during watering; and it deters unwelcome visitors like snails and ants setting up home in the container, where they can dine on organic matter and bonsai roots. In addition, it helps to prevent roots growing through the holes.

Once the screening is in place, from the outside insert a long copper wire into one hole, through the mesh and into the body of the container. Then take the other end of the copper wire and insert it, from the outside, into another hole, through the mesh and into the body of the container. If there is only one hole, wrap the wire around a small stick or galvanized nail to anchor it under the pot.

Line the bottom of the container with a shallow layer of gravel or very coarse soil. On top of it place a thin layer of peat moss or sphagnum moss to prevent soil from washing down and clogging the holes in the mesh. Add a soil mix appropriate to the plant (see pp. 49–51) and shape it into a mound or cushion. This is where the plant will be positioned. The anchor wires should stick up through the soil mix.

If potting is done at the optimum time, drastic pruning of both the root system and top growth can be done at the same time, but never prune roots without pruning top growth. Try to keep the proportional percentage the same: if you remove one-quarter of the top growth, you can safely remove one-quarter of the roots. (Balled and burlapped plants, having had some root damage from being recently dug, should be treated with somewhat more caution. Retain a greater percentage of root mass in proportion to top growth.)

If you are not potting at the optimum season, you can give the plant a very limited pruning of roots and top, but major pruning of any kind should wait.

For a day or so before potting the tree, allow the soil around it to dry a little to make removal from its pot easier. With tweezers or a blunt stick, remove any moss on the soil's surface and reserve it for future use. Remove the plant from its container and root prune as described on pp. 87–9. When removing the soil from around the roots, always stroke in the direction in which the roots grow, from the trunk outward and downward.

Planting the bonsai

When the bonsai is root pruned and the bottom plane of the rootball is flat, place the tree in its container. Placement in a pot is an important element in the critical success of the bonsai. In oblong pots, the tree traditionally is placed about one-third the distance away from one end; in round or square ones, it occupies the center as you look at the pot, but slightly to the rear of the center line.

The exceptions to this include weeping trees, in which the trunk should be planted closer to one side of the container, but not against it, so that it can cascade naturally over the opposite rim of the pot without visually over-balancing it. Cascades are placed so that the woody stem that undulates over the side is directly over a foot of the pot, although the exact placement is determined by the overall harmony of the pot and the plant.

A deeper pot than usual is needed for cascades and semicascades. Their rootballs are minimal, but their leaders and branches are large and lean heavily to one side, which can tend to unbalance the pots in which they reside. The deeper pot anchors the center of gravity of the bonsai and prevents plant and/or pot from toppling over.

Bonsai differ from houseplants in that as the latter are moved to a pot a size larger, bonsai are most often moved to a pot a size smaller, to suit the size of the bonsai and its condition. The smaller-size pot helps to keep the plant dwarf and develop a shallow, compact root system that in essence is forever young, thereby keeping the plant healthy and vigorous.

Place the tree on the off-center mound of soil, using a twisting motion to eliminate air pockets in the soil. Hold it with one hand, and check whether you think its position is correct. Keep the base of the trunk higher than the rim of the pot. With your other hand, add the soil and work it into, under and around the root system, firming the soil by jabbing it gently into place with a chopstick, moving it back and forth repeatedly to eliminate air pockets. They present a real danger to bonsai by offering favorable conditions for root rot. This also encourages better contact between roots and soil, and helps to prevent you damaging the roots through the pressure of your hands or another tool. A small trowel or flat level, for example, when applied too firmly, can affect the ability of the plant to absorb water through its roots, and then transport it onto the leaves (the scientific name for this is translocation). This process is vital to the life of the tree, and therefore nothing must interfere with it. For that reason, the only time to apply any deliberate pressure to the soil is when you want to control the growth of a large-leafed tree.

Keep adding soil until you can get no more around the root system, then, with the tree in place, twist the copper wires together diagonally across the rootball to secure the plant. Once the wires are loosely tied, add tiny rubber pads between the roots and the wires to act as cushions and prevent root damage from contact with the copper. Twist the two ends of the copper wire round each other a bit tighter, just tightly enough to steady the tree, and then bend the tiny ends downward. In a few seasons, when the wires are no longer needed to keep the plant in the pot, they can easily be cut through and then discarded. Then, holding the pot firmly with one hand, make a fist with your other hand and thump gently but firmly on the sides of the container. The soil will settle down even more.

Level the surface of the soil and brush away the excess. Leave a space of about $\frac{1}{4}$ inch between the soil level and the lip of the container. There should be a slight downward slope to the soil from the base of the tree to the rim of the container to facilitate drainage.

Large roots that break the surface of the soil occasionally need anchoring. Cut a 3 inch piece of copper wire thick enough to hold the root in place and bend it into a hairpin shape. Firm it down over the root and pin it down into the soil. Small, fine roots that surface can be pruned, but if the roots that pop up are large and worthy of display, adding a look of age and stability to the tree, or if they hold the potential of doing so, keep them exposed and let them develop further.

Sprinkle the soil lightly with room-temperature water. Then sprinkle the surface soil with dried, powdered or fresh moss and/or lichens. Work it in between the surface roots, leaving the upper surfaces of the roots visible to add to the illusion of age (see pp. 66–7). Powdered moss takes longer than fresh to turn green but eventually it makes a very smooth, lush, green carpet.

Kanuma Bonsai Park, Japan. Moss is an important ground cover in Japan, particularly in moist areas like Kyoto, hence its use in bonsai. No garden is considered complete without moss, and moss squares are laid in new gardens, in much the same way as turf is used in the West. In drier areas, such as Tokyo, it is more difficult to grow successfully, and it also suffers here from pollution. When you are choosing mosses for use in bonsai, try to select local varieties since these will be better able to withstand local conditions.

Cascades and semicascades, in particular, must be firmly wired into their containers. To improve the stability of these bonsai, add a fairly generous layer of gravel or stones to the bottom of the pot. This not only helps anchor the pot and the bonsai but also provides excellent drainage for a tall pot in which – for a dwarf plant – there is quite a lot of soil.

Watering

The bonsai is now ready to be watered for the first time. In preparation, lightly sprinkle the newly planted soil surface with water, to weight down the small pieces of fresh moss and to help fix the dried moss to the soil. This will prevent them from floating away in their first deep watering, just in case the water level in the watering pan is too high.

Fill the watering pan with room temperature water just high enough to reach under the rim of the bonsai container. Slowly place the container in the water. It will quickly soak up the water through the holes in the bottom of the container. At the first sign of darkening patches on the soil's surface, take the container out of the pan and place it in a protected area in the shade. Mist the foliage lightly.

Do not water again for a day or so. Freshly pruned roots cannot absorb moisture and nutrients with their usual facility until new roots grow out. The second time you water your bonsai, allow a gentle stream of water to trickle down the area immediately around the trunk. This area, the highest soil point of the bonsai, is the first to drain, the first to dry out, and it will be the last to absorb water from the bottom of the container. Watch the bonsai carefully. The look of dry soil around the trunk will also let you know that the roots have once again begun to function smoothly.

Repotting

Repotting has many purposes, all of which help to maintain the health of a bonsai.

Repotting replenishes the soil with nutrients, and also improves its texture; this, in turn, encourages feeding and rooting. It brings fresh soil to the bonsai, which will improve the tree's health. When you repot, you change the soil in the container before the roots have a chance to fill the container, which would prevent the soil from functioning properly. In short, you stop the bonsai becoming root-bound, the condition that results when roots grow so thickly that they cannot take the sustenance they need from the soil. Repotting is also a way to restructure the configuration of the entire root system.

In time, every healthy bonsai will fill its container with roots. The length of time it takes to do this varies considerably with the type of tree, its vitality, growing stage, fertilizing program, soil mix, and much more. Generally, however, a young tree in the active growing stage should be transplanted once a year and a mature tree, once every two or three years.

More specifically, flowering plants, fruiting trees, and bamboo are normally repotted every year, and broad-leafed evergreen and deciduous trees, once every two years. All conifers, especially pines, are exceptions, since they need repotting only once every four or five years. Bonsai, however, do not always grow according to plan and you should, therefore, check every year for rootbound conditions, and repot accordingly.

In repotting try to retain the very typical white mold which grows symbiotically with healthily growing pines and hornbeams. This mold, found on both the tree and in the soil, provides benefits that uncontaminated soil cannot. It is proof of active growth. The secret to keeping it alive is to maintain the tree at a temperature that allows the soil to be slightly moist during the day but dry at night. This gives the tree new vitality.

The five-needled pine should be repotted and pruned in spring when its needles are about to burst and at the end of summer when the buds are hard. If it is repotted at this time, it will have white mold growing over its drainage holes after just ten days. It is a signal that the tree has taken root. Even if the roots are damaged, they secrete a resin that will help to heal the pruning wounds. When repotting, the mold should be broken up into fine particles, then mixed into the new soil.

When done at the proper time of the year, and done carefully so that enough soil is left for the rootball, repotting is not a problem. Up to a third of the soil can be removed if it is done just as the buds swell but before the needles break during the spring growth spurt.

To repot, simply take the tree out of the container in late winter or early spring, before active spring growth starts, and examine the rootball. Note whether or not the tree needs repotting, then put it back in its container. When buds appear and roots are actively growing, stimulated by warmth and increased light, repot.

Keep the bonsai on the dry side and try to work in a shady, non-windy place, on a calm, cloudy day. Carefully cut the wire that holds the tree in its container. Then gently remove the ground cover and keep it in reserve. Take the tree from its pot. If the drainage material sticks to the bottom, shake it off on a piece of newspaper or a paper plate. Remove the wire mesh screening, putting it, along with the copper wire and the container, in hot, soapy water.

Unravel the tangle of roots. Take 1–2 inches of soil from the rootball. Cut any strong tap root that might have sprouted and shorten the old tap root, some of which may be left from the original potting. Newly developed running roots should be pruned to encourage the growth of fine roots closer to the trunk base. Beneath the trunk there may be an accumulation of old soil and old or rotted roots. Remove them by gouging or scraping them out, leaving a hollow space. If there is a fairly large space without roots, encourage new growth in that area by applying a rooting hormone formulated specifically for woody plants.

During this traumatic time, moisture content in the soil is important: it should be neither dry nor soggy. Moisten it just enough so that it holds together loosely in a crumbly lump when you squeeze it in your hand.

When the tree has been root-pruned and is again in place in its container, backfill with the fresh soil and settle it into the pot and around the roots just as you did at its original potting. After watering as before, put it in the shade for about two weeks.

Root pruning and repotting

1 *The mass of roots, many of which have reached the edge of the container, are ample proof that this tree needs root pruning, and then repotting.*

2 *Remove the soil from around the roots, and tease out the roots with a chopstick or other blunt stick or with a special bonsai root rake, available from bonsai nurseries.*

3 *Cut thick roots with root pruners, making sure that you cut them so that they have a flat base on which to sit; this will make the tree easier to repot.*

4 *Finer roots should be cut back by about a third, both round the sides of the rootball and underneath. Use fine long-handled snippers for this job.*

5 *Clean and pasteurize the container, and place fine mesh over the drainage holes to prevent the layer of gravel slipping through. Insert anchorage wires through the holes.*

6 *Add an appropriate soil mix round the roots of the tree, then replace any gravel or moss, and water gently. Keeping the bonsai warm will encourage new root growth.*

Chapter 6
Special Techniques

Root. Rock. Mountain. Raft. Forest. These may, at first sight, seem inappropriate in a book about the art of bonsai and bonsai trees. As well as containing all the necessary technical information, however, this is also a book about the philosophy of bonsai. For the world of bonsai is a good deal larger than a mere root or mountain. It has to do with nature and God, birth and death, and the history and geography of China and Japan. To understand bonsai is to understand roots and rocks and mountains – and man.

Bonsai represents a very close bond between the here and the hereafter, and has all manner of religious and esthetic overtones. What results is something that can hopefully be called "truth" and "beauty". The Chinese and Japanese see these qualities in man's constantly evolving relationship with God – and nature.

The magnitude of nature's influence is such that it is humanizing to be able to view the natural phenomena on a smaller, more relative, scale. Hence bonsai, and hence root and rock and mountain, and more.

This chapter will give you the basics of many techniques special to bonsai, encompassing the creation of forests, rafts, clinging-to-rock bonsai, and *saikei*, and will tell you how to care for, and how to display, them.

Juniperus chinensis "Sargentii" Sargent juniper
This Sargent juniper is about 350 years old, and was found growing in the wild in 1930s. It is a unique example of the driftwood style and formed part of the Japanese Garden at Expo 70 in Osaka. Here the dead wood twists toward the sky, giving an impression of movement. In addition, the bleached white of the dead wood provides a stunning contrast to the reddish-brown of the curved trunk and the dense compact foliage. Known colloquially as "Flying Dragon", this bonsai is part of the Ueda Collection, Japan.

Forests

Forests, or group plantings, are among the most dramatic representations of the art of bonsai. To the novice, they are romantic and mysterious. To the expert, they are triumphs of know-how and technique. At the very least, they evoke intense feeling.

Viewing a well-composed forest is like looking into the primeval woods: it is not difficult to imagine birds singing in the branches, deer prancing into the clearing, and magnificent sunrises and sunsets glinting through the finely branched limbs. How can you create such an illusion? Basically it results from a combination of skills, imagination, and artistry.

The process has to start with numbers. Two, three, five, seven, nine trees, and more, in odd increments, dignify the Japanese people's profound respect for those numbers. A knowledgeable bonsaiist would never use four or six trees in a composition; those numbers are simply not part of the bonsai vernacular.

Then, select trees of the same species; only on rare occasions do bonsaiists combine plants of different kinds in a forest group. Purists go so far as to use seedlings from only one parent, waiting for at least one growing season to pass before planting so they can be sure that the trees are closely alike in habit and characteristics.

A bonus in the eyes of many forest growers is that the "perfect" tree, with exactly the correct branch and trunk configuration, is not a prerequisite. Since every tree used will be one of many (sometimes more than twenty), the individual qualities are somewhat less important than in the formal styles that use only a single specimen. In fact, when several generations of plants – including an obviously aged specimen – are used, properly positioned, the effect can be even more dramatic.

The greater the diameter of the trunk, the taller the tree should be. If the tallest tree becomes the focus of the planting, therefore, its diameter should be the greatest and the surrounding trees will descend incrementally in both diameter and height. In addition, the shorter the tree, the fewer branches it should support.

Whether you are using evergreen or deciduous material, placement in a forest is critical and should afford a clear view of each tree from the front and both sides. In every view, the grouping should represent its forest home and the trees' struggle for light. As in any struggle, some fare better than others, and small, perhaps scrawny, examples should not be excluded from the whole. Also, as in nature, there should be trees at varying stages of development.

In the interests of realism, the positioning of each tree is of the utmost importance. A forest bonsai always assumes asymmetrical proportions when viewed from the front,

Stewartia monodelpha
Stewartia
A forest planting, this was created by Saburo Kato and forms part of the Mansei-en Collection, Japan. Although stewartias are common trees in Japan, and have been used there in bonsai for many years, they have only recently started to become common in bonsai in the West. Fine-textured, low-growing plants, such as mosses, and some heathers and ferns as here, are all suitable for use as ground cover. Not only do they help to anchor the soil in the container, they also increase the naturalism and visual impact of the overall design.

Picea jezoensis *Edo spruce*
This large bonsai forest from the Oguchi Collection in Japan was created from two 220-year-old spruces during the 1980s. It is a supreme example of the bonsaiist breaking the conventions: normally a large tree with a thick trunk would be accompanied by a medium-size tree rather than the small one used to create the interesting juxtaposition here. Also, although two trees can clearly be successful in a planting, even numbers are generally avoided, certainly up to nine. In spite of the small amount of soil on the slab base, both trees retain their stability and vigor.

having one long side with a gentle but noticeable slant, and a short side with a far steeper slant. What results is an acute-angled triangle, which must be arranged to suit the shape of the container you are using. Within this triangle, the long, straight trunks should give way to a proportionate amount of branching: the more trunks involved, the fewer branches are needed for asymmetrical balance.

Finding the right stock for the effect you want is always rather hit and miss – you can be sure that if you have a preconceived idea of what you want, you will not be able to find it. As a result, many bonsaiists who work with group styles ultimately raise their own stock, starting with seedlings. They put these seedlings into training immediately, with straight trunks and fine branching the goals from the start. Bonsaiists rarely plant a forest of untrained

stock unless the trees are extremely young, and even then only after a year or two in their own nurseries.

First, make sure the trunks are straight, then train the outer branches only (remember that the configuration of the composition may change, and the outer branches may be the only ones that remain). You should, however, leave the majority of inner branches in place until you are absolutely sure of their fate. Leaving more branches on as long as possible brings an added benefit, since the more dependent branches there are on the trees, the thicker the trunks will grow.

Since the scale of the forest planting is so minute, try not to use plants that fruit. It would be most incongruous to see a group of fifteen small trees burdened with huge peaches or apples hanging from bent branches. If you must have a

GROUP STYLES

Creating a forest

1 *Choose trees of different heights and with different-sized trunks. Plan out the composition in advance, placing the taller trees to the front.*

2 *Try to avoid placing any trees on the same line, either front to back or side to side. Use moss and gravel to help anchor both soil and trees in the container.*

3 *After planting, give the trees their first pruning as a group, eliminating any branches that impinge on their neighbors, and any that detract from the overall effect.*

Raft style

1 *Nursery grown conifers are ideal for training as rafts, since their bushy growth enables you to choose which branches to eliminate and which to retain.*

2 *Remove all the surplus growth from the underside and top of the tree, then wire those branches that you wish to train to become the new individual trees.*

3 *Bury the rootball and trunk in a fairly deep container in a suitable soil mix until roots have sprouted from the base of each branch, now an individual tree.*

fruiting composition, make your choice from among the smaller fruited varieties such as cherry, holly, or one of the many-colored varieties of *Pyracantha*.

Planting a forest

Plant the forest when the roots of the trees are more than adequate to maintain the tree but not fully mature. Dig the trees from the nursery bed or carefully knock them from their pots. Prune them very lightly, eliminating only weak branches and those that lack substance and grace. Carefully remove the soil from the tender roots, probing gently with a chopstick and wiggling it back and forth. If the tap root is long, clip it back with root pruners. Prune the smaller roots, too, but by no more than one-third their length.

Prepare the container (see pp. 89–90), then position the main tree – that is, the largest. A useful rule of thumb is to place it one-third of the distance in from one end. Behind it, and slightly to the right and left, go the second and third trees, with the fourth and fifth added alongside them. After these principal trees are in position, fill in with the balance of the seedlings, being careful to compose them into as natural a grouping as possible. Plan to place the smallest, thinnest seedling nearest the edge of the container.

As you go, spread the roots of each tree toward the center and the edges of the container, trying not to bunch any roots together. Also avoid overlapping the roots since they do not appreciate competition, especially at this stage. After you have fitted the roots together like the pieces of a jigsaw puzzle, gradually begin to add your soil mix. (Depending on the size of the trees you have chosen, you might find it necessary to anchor the seedlings with wire to stop them moving while their roots are establishing themselves.) Use the chopstick to firm soil gently around the roots. Water the composition, using a fine rosette on the watering can just to dampen the soil. Then, sprinkle a dusting of finely sieved peat around the roots. This serves to anchor the covering of sphagnum moss, which you should add to help retain moisture while the trees become used to their new surroundings. After that, the forest is ready for a thorough watering.

Until the miniature forest settles down, keep it in a protected area where the sun will not scorch it and where water is nearby. Do not even contemplate wiring until the trees are firmly rooted in place, which could take six months to a year, again depending on the plants you have used. At that point, begin whatever wiring you feel the forest needs, finally removing the sphagnum moss and planting real moss and lichens.

Raft style

The raft style is unusual, and found only occasionally in nature. It occurs when a live tree is, for some reason, uprooted and falls to the earth. Many of the branches on the lower side break as the tree hits the ground and, as a result, the nodes at the base of the branches come into contact with the soil and have a chance to develop roots. When this occurs, the branches remaining on what is now the exposed upper part of the trunk continue to grow, to reach for the light and, eventually, to become individually rooted trees themselves, still linked, however, by the mother trunk.

The Japanese follow this sequence of events in creating what they call raft-style bonsai, also called root-connected or straight-line style. In this technique, the trunk of a single tree is laid down so that it is horizontal and partially buried. The branches, rising upward from the main trunk, are then trained as trees.

In creating a raft, you are obviously limited as to the placement of these new "trees" since you have to work with the branching arrangement that exists. However, a judicious initial choice of plant will help you to create a natural effect.

Select a tree whose rootball is not very large, and which has the majority of its branches on one side of the trunk. Ideally, a graduated group of at least five branches is recommended for maximum effectiveness, with the smallest branches at one end. Fewer than five branches will tend to look insignificant.

Any curves in the trunk should be positioned toward the back of the composition. This will increase the feeling of depth and perspective so important to the grouping. Now prune the unnecessary or undesirable branches from both the top and underneath parts of the raft. These include those branches that are crossing other branches, and those that are skimpy, as well as any that are not in sympathy with the rest of the grouping. At this point do any wiring necessary (see pp. 84–5), tackling each remaining branch individually. By doing this, you can easily manipulate those branches to your taste, while leaving the surrounding branches undisturbed.

Remove the bark from the underside of the trunk, directly on and to either side of a node. The area you remove may measure between $\frac{1}{2}$–1 inches in length and should span about one-third of the circumference of the trunk. Use a sharp, sterile knife. Wet the exposed areas immediately, then apply a light dusting of hormone rooting powder specifically formulated for woody plants.

Depending on the size of the tree, find or build a box that will accommodate both the original root and the trunk placed horizontally, and plant the trunk to approximately half its depth in sandy soil. Try to tease out as much of the soil from the top half of the rootball as you can, and flatten it enough to be able to bury the roots in a mound of soil that is not so high as to be completely out of scale. Insert holding pins to insure the bonsai is stable in the box.

With the original tree root buried in soil, you can carry on feeding the plant uninterrupted, and its remaining branches can continue to grow upward. In time, and with adequate feeding, watering and general care, the nodes and part of the trunk that touch the soil will develop their own roots, just as the tree does in nature, thereby creating a group of trees that have their own root systems and could lead their own lives. Eventually, those original branches will look like a grove of aged trees, growing independently, yet together.

Keep your raft-in-training in a relatively sunny position, since the branches have live needles or leaves which must have sun to produce the food vital to its survival. Also, make sure it never dries out and is positioned firmly on its bench in its box. Roots will have sprouted from the exposed parts of the trunk between one and two years after preparation. If you are at all uncertain about the root development, leave the tree in its rooting box a little longer – with bonsai, patience is a virtue! When you are as sure as it is possible to be that an adequate root system has developed, remove the front of the box. From the removal of this one side, you can determine if the raft is ready to be planted in a shallow pot, or whether it needs a slightly deeper container to encourage an even sturdier root system.

Remove all the wiring and let the branches grow as they will for the rest of the season. Then, confident that the raft can support itself with its new root system, carefully cut the original root from the end of the tree. At the appropriate time for repotting (see pp. 92–3) reassess the form and direction of the new bonsai, rewiring as you think necessary. To increase the girth of the branches, pinch out the new growth to one bud.

Depth and perspective cannot be emphasized enough, for even with small branches, indeed, small trees, you can achieve a feeling of distance by exploiting carefully the raft's own characteristics. Since illusion is everything, use whatever tricks you think necessary to create the feeling of varying distances in a small space. You might, for instance, try to use the tallest branches (those closest to the original rootball) as your "close-up" branches, with the interme-diate branches as the center, and the shortest branches as the farthest points of your composition. An alternative is to place the tallest branch in front, with the intermediate branches in the middle and the shortest to the rear of the container. As you become more experienced with this technique, you will probably create some interesting alternatives of your own.

The Japanese, reputedly, equated the look of this tree with that of a raft, which is visibly supported by a series of horizontal beams emanating from one large main beam.

Root over rock

There are various forms within bonsai that bring together trees and rocks. One is called, simply, root over rock or (the Japanese term) stone-clasping style. In this style a plant with long, thin roots is either grown *over* a rock, clinging fast to its rough, craggy surfaces, or *in* a rock, where tiny man-made indentations serve as planting holes.

Since bonsai is a scaled-down representation of nature, the rock (or mountain) should be much larger proportion-ally than the tree that grows tenaciously from its ledges.

Planting in rock

1 *Position the roots of your chosen tree so that they will fall into the natural crevices of the rock. Use a little "muck" (see p. 102) to hold them in place.*

2 *If the tree's roots are not long enough to reach the container initially, wrap the rootball and rock tightly with twine to prevent roots sprouting out sideways.*

3 *Wrap the rootball in plastic and bury it in a deep container filled with sand. This will encourage long, branching roots to grow. Then, plant the tree in the rock.*

LEFT: Juniperus procumbens *"Nana" Dwarf Chinese juniper This forty-year-old Chinese juniper has been trained as a rock-clasping bonsai for nearly thirty years. Planted in an oval black and blue glazed container, it is 10 inches high.*

The Kiso River, north of Kyoto. Typical of much of the remaining countryside of Japan, this area has furnished many bonsai (particularly Japanese cedars from the slopes of the mountains), as well as garden stones from the riverbanks.

Alternatively, rocks can suggest kinder, less precipitous circumstances, portraying an island or plateau, or a rill or hill with a longer, flatter shape.

For the novice, rocks suitable for this style can be found in nurseries with a good range of rock-garden plants or in specialist bonsai nurseries. You may also find rocks that seem appropriate in the wild, but remember that in many places, including country parks and beaches, it is illegal to remove rocks.

Choose a roughly textured stone since it will have a desirable weathered look, and also because it is easier to establish a plant on a surface that can both hold soil and give roots something to grasp. Also, choose a rock with a surface that is appropriately flattened on its bottom-most plane. Use a saw and sandpaper to smooth out bumps and projections, if necessary.

If the scene you choose to depict is based on a mountain range miles away, the plants you choose should be that much smaller than the rock and should also show all the positive and negative aspects of your stone. Conversely, if the scene is a closeup, you have the opportunity to hide the rock's imperfections with an array of trees, shrubs, mosses, and lichens.

It is wise, at first, to use plants that are readily available and native to your area. Since scale and proportion are so vital to the success of your root-over-rock bonsai, select a small-leafed or needled plant.

The proper time to create your bonsai depends on the kind of plants you use. Generally, try to plant just before bud-burst in spring, although some needled evergreens will take planting in fall. A rule of thumb for scheduling is to decide on the time at which the least amount of damage and disruption will be suffered by the tree; a time when you know growth is about to surge; and a time when weather conditions are expected to be kindest.

Choosing a suitable container is often a concern, but it need not be. Any bonsai container of shallow proportions is a likely candidate (although, obviously, you should avoid a container that might detract visually from the rock planting). However, if your plants are shallow-rooted, you may want to pot it deeply for six months to a year to encourage more and lengthier root growth. When the growth is finally long enough, carefully remove the plant from the soil and wash the roots clean.

Planting on rock
The materials to have on hand are milled and unmilled sphagnum moss, pasteurized topsoil, a small quantity of unmixed perlite and vermiculite, slender annealed copper wire cut in 3–4 inch lengths and bent in half to look like hairpins, lead fishing or drape weights in small sizes, hammer, awl, and a bucket of tepid water.

Combine the first three ingredients in equal parts. To this mix add enough water to make it hold together in a ball. Knead it and try to press as much air from the mix as possible. This product – muck – acts as a clay-like, sticky fixative, making a bed for the roots and establishing a medium through which they can absorb all the water and nutrients they need.

Root-over-rock bonsai necessitate some special techniques. Decide what will be the front of your plant and rock. Make sure that the rock is wet before you begin work. Study your bare-rooted tree, pruning the minute roots carefully and preserving as much of the longer roots as possible. A light pruning will encourage root ramification which will eventually make the bonsai hold fast to the surface of the rock.

Study the grouping of the roots around the trunk; this will give you an idea of how they will fall naturally. Divide them into four (one each for front, back, right, and left). Decide which of the roots are visually most important to the composition, and try to retain as many main roots as possible. These will be the prominent features of the finished composition.

Using the awl and hammer, carve a tiny hole in the rock, at the same time making a small, graduated crevice on each side. Then firmly wedge the wire into the hole with a weight, bring the ends of the wire out of the hole and along the crevice, ready to receive a root. Repeat this procedure for each hole you plan. (Some bonsaiists use epoxy glue to hold the wiring in place, others have reservations about the effect of resins on bare roots and prefer to establish a firm foundation without using chemically based substances. However, much has been said in favor of this approach, so it may be worth experimenting with on small plants, if you prefer.)

"Smear" the holes and graduated crevices with muck, continuing to carve the slight crevice and to build the base of muck inside it, until you reach the container below. Cover the wire with milled sphagnum moss. Then position the bonsai where you think it should be and spread its roots directly down the paths of the crevices, embedding them in the muck. If the roots are long enough to reach the container, tuck the ends in and around the place where rock and container meet to protect them. Place muck along the trails where roots meet rock, and also where they wrap around the rock's base. Gently twist the wires around the roots, leaving enough room for growth. Cover the wired roots with another layer of unmilled sphagnum moss. Then water the bonsai from the bottom up, misting the leaves and roots, and taking care to insure that the muck and moss stay in place.

In-rock bonsai are actually planted in man-made or natural holes in the surface of the rock. If there are no holes in the rock, gouge or drill them, depending on the hardness of the rock. Drainage is generally not a problem since the hole will be shallow and water will evaporate quickly.

Line the hole with fine nylon mesh to prevent soil from spilling out. Follow this with a layer of fine gravel and soil, then position your plants. Add more soil and a topping of sphagnum moss.

Place the finished bonsai in the shade for several weeks and gradually expose it to more light – its final home will be in partial shade. Root-over-rock and in-rock bonsai are especially sensitive to the vagaries and vicissitudes of temperature and wind. It is wise, therefore, to monitor the moisture in the soil very carefully, watering the roots and misting the leaves or needles as often as two or three times a day, if warranted.

After about six months or so, the outer layer of sphagnum moss should be removed so that new, vigorously growing roots do not develop in the sphagnum. At the same time, the muck can be washed from the roots so that the paths of the roots down the rock are exposed.

If you buried the new bonsai in a deep container prior to placing it in its proper bonsai container, now is the time to remove and transplant it, being careful at all times not to damage the root structure. For the container housing the rock planting, use a muck solution around the rock and a slightly lighter mix with proportionally more soil and perhaps a little granulated charcoal for other plants, should you want to add some.

It takes time to get to know a bonsai. After about six months to a year, you will be well acquainted with its likes and dislikes. After you have been through every season, taking note of its reactions to the changing conditions, you will know even more.

An exception to the timetable above is the aged tree, newly introduced to a rock-clasping situation. With older plants, it could take years before the roots actually clasp the rock and you have the desired effect. Have patience. If the plants are suitable and the rock is distinctive, the goal is worth waiting for.

Although in bonsai, proportion is all important, you can see enormous variation in the relative sizes of rock and container in the outstanding collections around the world. Some root-over-rock bonsai grow on stones that all but fill their shallow containers, while others have ones that take up very little space. There are no hard and fast rules – beauty really is in the eyes of the beholder. It is always important to consider proportion, however, before you commit yourself to a specific tree-rock-container combination.

Saikei

Saikei (pronounced "sigh-kay") is a form of bonsai in which trained plant specimens are brought together in a realistic, proportionate interpretation of a landscape. Although it sounds simple, several horticultural skills are involved, all of which must work together to create a natural scene.

As far as plants are concerned, some of the smallest and youngest bonsai material can be used in *saikei*. Distinctive, and with some unique properties of their own, these plants can be the small, imperfect, material frequently rejected for traditional bonsai. They can be so small that ones reserved for *mame* bonsai can be used. Even seedlings, which are far from aged and branched, are appropriate.

Another distinct difference between *saikei* and the more familiar forms of bonsai is that the use of a variety of plants in one setting is more the norm than the exception. Since *saikei* is an attempt to translate a broad natural scene into miniature terms, the realistic use of different varieties of plants is necessary. However, *saikei* is not confined to the use of multiple plants, and there are justifiably famous examples which use a single, well-grown plant in the finished landscape.

This bonsai is planted in a tree stump, chosen – as in a rock planting – for its esthetic qualities and to complement the other plants. Providing enough water is the biggest problem; in this example from the Ueda Collection, that is partly solved by placing the planting in a pond in the garden.

It is important with *saikei* to use plants that require the same conditions. Without cultural similarities, the job of maintaining the health of the landscape can be an overwhelming, if not impossible, chore.

Involved in *saikei* too are the rocks, sand, shrubs, and accompanying plants common to both woodland and shore; in fact all the natural phenomena – streams, rivers, fallen trees, beaches, craggy outcroppings or ledges, waterfalls, ponds, marshes, and glades – can be captured in *saikei*. Your task is to combine all these elements with the trees, shrubs, mosses, and lichens into a harmonious whole, using material that will live together in one container.

The language used in *saikei* is the same as in traditional bonsai: the formal and informal, windswept and cascade styles are used; the scale and proportion of plants to each other and to the rock or rocks (it is not essential to use any rocks in a *saikei* composition and there are well-known examples in the bonsai world that do not; most, however, do feature one or more) is vital; and a harmonious overall effect is the goal.

In choosing rocks suitable for planting, look not only for distinctive, craggy rocks but also for those that have a meandering thread of white or beige coursing down their faces, to resemble a waterfall or stream. Keep a sharp eye out for a stone that looks like a hillside undulating downward in terrace after terrace, or a craggy rock with a generous plateau that could represent the meadow below a precipice in your final picture. Use whatever the rock can offer you as a head start toward realism.

ABOVE: *A clinging-to-rock bonsai from the Ueda Collection. Like the tree on p. 103, this is situated in the garden on a 10 foot long table carved from a single block of stone. The bonsai is turned periodically so that the plants grow evenly.*

OPPOSITE: *A* saikei *created at the Brooklyn Botanic Garden by Frank Okamura after a class by the leading practitioners of the form, Toshio Kawamoto and Tom Yamamoto. This example is composed of five different species:* Chamaecyparis obtusa *'Nana' (a dwarf variety of Hinoki cypress),* Chamaecyparis pisifera *'Snow' (a variety of Sawara cypress),* Juniperus chinensis *(Chinese juniper),* Rhododendron sp. *(a small-leafed azalea) and* Picea abies *'Maxwellii' (a dwarf variety of Norway spruce), as well as rocks and ground cover. Overall, this landscape measures 24 × 20 inches.*

105

Rocks for *saikei* plantings should be prepared in the same ways as for root-over-rock bonsai. Muck and wire, moss and awl are the tools and materials you need, and trays of clay or interesting stones, cement or wood are also desirable. Wash the soil from the roots, but take care to keep the rootball whole. Separate the roots into quadrants to ascertain where they will naturally fall. If you are using a variety of plants, select leaves, trunks, and branch positions that are in scale and color harmony with one another. When planning ground cover and accompanying plants, be sure that soil and rock will still be visible.

If the stone has been cast in the role of a mountain, the plants should be proportionally smaller. If not, the plants can dominate the scene, with the rock or rocks partially hidden beneath the soil, more nearly approximating the way rocks are found in nature.

Saikei offers an opportunity to use tiny horticultural gems. Mosses, lichens, and tiny violets kept even smaller by judicious pinching, grasses, miniature veronicas, and thymes are all possibilities, depending on the scene you are painting and the appropriateness of the plants to that scene. Some of these can be found growing wild in cities and in the countryside, and have the advantages of being native to the area, hardy to the climate, impervious to pollution and drought, and available at the lowest possible cost. (Never pick any protected wildflower species.)

As with other rock plantings, watering is essential. Keep *saikei* in dappled shade and water two or three times a day. Since drainage is quick and water-retention capabilities are at a minimum, this is imperative.

Outdoor display

The way bonsai are displayed is important for several reasons. First and most obvious, proper display will show the bonsai to its best advantage – it is rather like you being photographed on your best side for the best results. Next, its display can provide an added measure of safety from such dangers as visiting animals, both domestic and wild, and from the wind, which can easily knock a bonsai from its container or shelf. And, perhaps most important, the proper method of display will help to keep bonsai healthy.

Bonsai look most comfortable and natural in a garden, not competing against their garden-variety relations, which have grown to comparatively huge proportions, but against

Juniperus chinensis 'Sargentii'
Sargent juniper
Photographed at the Yonan-so Hotel, Utsunomiya, this Sargent juniper forms part of the Sudo Collection. A driftwood style bonsai, with a delicately curving trunk and bright green, fine-textured foliage, this is perfectly complemented by the "Moon and Clouds" scroll with which it is displayed. Sargent junipers are ideal for training in a variety of styles since they have very flexible trunks and branches that can be shaped without damage.

a neutral background. An effective backdrop could be as simple as the fencing surrounding the property; the wall of a garage, finished in a color that does not reflect light too strongly; a length of hanging bamboo or straw matting; a sheet of sprayed or stained marine plywood; a wall of cement blocks or plastic in a muted shade; a wall of non-flowering vines; or a hedge. In fact, the background for a collection has no bounds other than those of the imagination. The single unassailable rule that applies is that the background should be non-competitive and unobtrusive – no fuchsia pink or marine blue! Shades from off-whites to tans, from soft grays to pale blues, even some muted burnt oranges or golds, depending on the coloring of the bonsai to be exhibited, are all appropriate.

The majority of bonsai must have sun. The sun's heat accelerates loss of water from the plant, however, as well as increasing evaporation from the soil. And as the soil dries out, the roots will suffer. Consider, therefore, the amount, intensity, and direction of the sun that your collection will receive. It also follows that in spring and fall, when the strength of the sun is gentler and the plants are either putting out new growth or hardening off for the winter, full sun may be necessary. Good but tempered light is the key to maintaining a collection.

You can temper natural light by providing a "sun hat" for your collection. A simple roof made of snow fencing (lath strips attached to each other with galvanized wire) is both attractive and practical, providing direct sunlight that is cut by about 50 percent. In this way, the bonsai derive all the benefits of the sun's rays yet do not suffer from extremes of heat. The wind can also play havoc with a collection. A solution is to extend the snow fencing to hang down both sides of the "sun hat" and the back.

If the day is cloudy, roll the fencing up and fasten it in place with a piece of wire. If it is particularly windy or brutally hot and sunny, roll it down for added protection. It serves as an outdoor, indestructible shade.

In situations where this kind of structure is impossible, an exposure that takes advantage of the sun for a few hours, with shade or partial shade following, is advisable. A predominantly eastern exposure, with southern sun toward midday, would probably be self-regulating.

On what should bonsai sit? Basically, on anything secure. A wide variety of options is available, ranging from tables to benches, from wooden or plastic shelving resting on cement blocks or bricks to elaborate stepped benches that house the smallest bonsai on the highest and narrowest shelf and the largest on the lowest and widest shelf. Stone and stucco walls built with cantilevered ledges of local stone have been designed to hold bonsai; tall pillars of sand-cast cement designed to be planted firmly in the earth can hold cascades aloft for effective viewing; and shortened versions of the same pillars have been created for the viewing of formal uprights and forests. Generally, though, a successful bonsaiist does not need acres of property and an abundance of time and money with which to shower his or her collection. What *is* needed is information about and dedication to that collection.

People in the most inhospitable of circumstances have raised and maintained beautiful bonsai – in city centers, on balconies and roof terraces; on houseboats; in the steamy tropics and in the coldest parts of the world, through both summer and winter. The important point is that they have found a way to provide their trees with sun, air and water in the amounts most appropriate to the plants they have chosen. What is often most difficult for the new bonsaiist to understand is that bonsai are really sturdy plants and are bound to flourish under the correct conditions.

Bonsai can be displayed as a collection or as individual specimens. In a collection, the trees should be placed with enough room around them so they do not infringe on the viewability or environment of their neighbors. On the other hand, they should not be solitary statements in enormous spaces that reduce the bonsai to insignificance.

Bonsai can be brought inside to lend grace to a special occasion. They can remain indoors, even in the dead of winter, for a day or two. Spending the night inside in an unheated room would be most beneficial, but they should be returned to their cold environment before growth and sap are prematurely encouraged into activity.

At all times, but especially if you take them indoors for a time, bonsai should be shown at eye level. In a living-room, a hall, and a dining-room, eye level can mean differing heights. Take care to exhibit your bonsai at the best height in any given situation. By far the most offensive breach of judgment is to force admirers to view bonsai from above. Bonsai should never be looked down upon, but elevated to an appropriate height.

The display of bonsai, whether a single example or a large collection, can be left to the imagination. Without good horticultural practices, however, all the imagination in the world, even the budget to match, will not produce a collection that excites the senses and emotions with increasing intensity and respect as the years go by. And that would be a shame, since it is one of the fundamental joys of working with bonsai in the first place.

107

Chapter 7
Indoor Bonsai

Once you are intrigued by, and have some knowledge of and commitment to bonsai, probably the severest punishment is to be separated from your trees in winter, which many climates in the world force to one degree or another.

Happily, the cultivation of indoor bonsai can dispel the gloom and keep alive the inner satisfaction that pruning, wiring, watering, feeding, repotting, and watching bring.

As far as material for indoor cultivation is concerned, there is no scarcity of choice. Any plant that would not weather a winter outside yet develops a woody structure as it matures, and has merit as a bonsai, is a potential subject. The distinct difference that characterizes the growing of these plants as indoor bonsai is the total control that you have to exercise over the tree in every area of its cultivation. From conditions of light to those of shade, from heat to lack of it, from humidity to dryness, soil and nutrients, you now have more to do with creating the environment than does nature.

Certainly the plant must have the conditions that fit its own special needs — whether it turns out to be a positive experience or a disaster depends entirely on the caretaker. Contrary to widely held beliefs, however, growing bonsai indoors is not easier or harder than growing them outdoors — it's just different.

The best way to learn about the plants most appropriate to indoor bonsai cultivation is to visit the noted collections, nurseries, and greenhouses in your part of the world. This chapter will tell you how to care for that plant.

Cotoneaster microphyllus *var.* thymifolius *Cotoneaster*
This informal upright bonsai was started from a rooted cutting by
Frank Okamura at the Brooklyn Botanic Garden twenty-seven years
ago. Its container is oval green and glazed, and measures $5 \times 3\frac{1}{2}$ inches,
by $1\frac{1}{2}$ inches high. Overall, the bonsai measures $6 \times 4\frac{1}{2}$ inches, and is
7 inches high.

First considerations

There are literally hundreds of plants from which to choose for indoor cultivation. The wide range of material recognized as woody stemmed and trunked tropicals and semi-tropicals, which in many climate zones fit into the euphemistic grouping called "houseplants", are ripe for bonsai training. You have to remember, however, that although they are houseplants in one particular region, they are outdoor garden plants in another.

Even within the realm of indoor bonsai, there are interesting differences. It has become so natural a part of the art that some bonsaiists not only have extensive indoor collections, but within that group have created subgroups, keeping some plants inside throughout the year, and giving others an outdoor hiatus during the warmest part of the growing season, bringing them in well before cool temperatures and dull light change their environment.

One important point to remember about indoor bonsai which remain indoors, forgoing an outdoor summer vacation, is that they are also protected from a battery of unfamiliar and potentially devastating insects and diseases. Theoretically if, while outside, an "enemy" invaded their territories – soil, leaf, or wood – it could go undetected. The affected bonsai would then be reintroduced indoors with the disease or insect silently at work. With none of the natural combatants that nature provides permanent outdoor dwellers to rely on, the bonsai could then be dealt a fatal blow by their unseen attacker.

Whenever a new or an "outdoor" plant is introduced to the indoor collection, therefore, it should be kept in isolation for a period of two to three weeks before joining the established collection. This simple precaution can substantially reduce the likelihood of spreading disease or insects to the rest of the collection.

Light

On the question of light, the considerations are the same indoors as out (see p. 107), and your aim is to maximize available natural light, or to create it artificially. While natural light comes through all the windows, the intensity of that light is greatly reduced by the window itself, dirt and all, and by the size and angle of the window, which influence how long and how far the light will be able to enter. Light quality is also affected by the absorptive or reflective surroundings inside the room.

The distance the bonsai is placed from the window will bear greatly on how it fares and whether it will flower, fruit, or cone as expected, since the intensity of light varies according to its closeness to the source.

As with houseplants, the available light also depends on the season. In the fall, light is still rather strong but on the wane, so a place in a bright window will suit sun-loving plants. As the winter settles in, natural light dims and what was once a very bright exposure dims too. For bonsai that need only low light levels, this is not dangerous, but for others, it can be, which makes this the time to consider additional sources of light.

There are several possibilities. Fluorescent lighting, which varies from long, slender tubes to the newer and smaller circular types, all of which must be fitted into a fixture designed solely for fluorescent light, offers one suitable solution. Fluorescent lighting fixtures, however, are not known for their beauty and you may not want to use them if your bonsai will be included in the "public" areas of your home.

Many bonsaiists have constructed their own indoor bonsai trollies made of wooden supports and shelving, with fluorescent lights attached to the underside of each shelf so they can shine down on the plants below. Others have built tall "light boxes" from attractively stained, painted or papered wooden boxes, equipped with all the necessary electrical fittings. The boxes are situated on the floor or hang from the wall, depending on their size, and can be turned – rather like hi-fi speakers – to face the plants they are serving.

Still other growers prefer to keep their bonsai in a separate space altogether – such as a basement, attic, garage, or even an enclosed balcony – which makes everything, including lighting, a little easier. What is made more difficult by opting for this approach, obviously, is the appreciation of the collection. Either singly or in small groups, the bonsai have to be brought into the living areas to be admired and then returned to their habitat after a suitable interval.

OPPOSITE: Chamaecyparis obtusa *"Nana Gracilis"* Hinoki false cypress *Estimated to be about forty years old, this twin-trunk informal upright was in training for twenty years before being planted* *in its rectangular brown unglazed container. A slow-growing, dwarf cultivar popular in the West, this bonsai measures about 20 × 16 inches overall, and is 32 inches high.*

Generally speaking, two fluorescent tubes, usually white and warm-white, placed no more than 6 inches away from the plants and on for 18 hours a day at most, provide sufficient light to keep the majority of bonsai in good health. Of course, wherever they are placed, bonsai should be given a quarter turn each week to encourage balanced growth.

Since providing adequate light can become difficult in family living areas, try to combine natural with artificial light to maximize the benefits to the bonsai.

The object, after all, is to approximate most closely the original conditions that nurtured the plants. And, while you are doing that, you should also remember that even though conditions may be close, the bonsai are being grown in small pots and in small quantities of soil which dry out quickly. Just as extra protection from the cold will serve the plants well, so will extra protection from hot sunny days, both winter and summer.

Temperature

There are literally hundreds of plants that grow happily in what could be considered indoor conditions. Since, however, the definition of indoor in one area of the world is outdoor in another, you should do some research on potential plants and their growing needs before you try to establish them indoors.

In dealing with plants, there are a few groupings among which to look first: the plants that are native to your immediate indoor and outdoor climates, as well as those plants categorized as both tropicals and semi-tropicals. All of them can, to at least a certain degree, be grown indoors if the conditions, within reason, reproduce their outdoor needs.

If you are going to use local outdoor material as indoor bonsai, it must first, of course, become acclimatized to lower light levels, and to a change in temperature, before being introduced to its new home. A stay of about three to four weeks in the shade is sufficient, if it is begun before outdoor temperatures start to drop with the change of season.

In working with temperature and indoor bonsai, there are no specific rules of thumb. Temperatures must closely approximate those which are native to the plants. Tropicals, therefore, need fairly constant temperatures of between 60 and 75°F, since that is the range they would normally experience all year round if they were growing outdoors.

OPPOSITE: Leptospermum *sp.*
Australian 'tea' tree
A twin-trunk bonsai with beautiful pink flowers and small, crowded leaves, this was trained from a rooted cutting, and planted in its present rectangular brown unglazed container in 1975. Overall, the bonsai measures 6½ × 6½ inches, and is 10 inches high. It is native to Australia, New Zealand and Malaysia, and as such is very suitable for indoor cultivation.

Rhododendron indicum
Satsuki azalea
This beautiful informal upright is from the Sudo Collection in Japan. Although its blossoms are delicate, the bonsai itself conveys great strength, largely through the impressive trunk.

The scroll in the background depicts a swallow being blown by the wind, a perfect complement since swallows nest at the time the plant blooms. (Photographed at the Yonan-so Hotel, Utsunomiya, scroll by courtesy of Mrs Nakamura.)

114

Generally speaking, most tropicals (see Chapter 8) thrive in a temperature that does not dip too far below 60°F at night. This drop in temperature is a typical need of most plants. In fact, it is an accepted part of plantcare that most plants require a drop of at least 10 Fahrenheit degrees in temperature at night.

The treatment of plants depends on the area to which they are native. By definition, subtropical plants are used to less-than-tropical conditions and therefore require consistently cooler temperatures, usually around 42–60°F. During their artificially produced winter season, they thrive in temperatures of up to 54°F during the day and down to 42°F at night. This noticeable dip provides them with a time to rest and recuperate from manufacturing food, growing, and flowering.

Appropriate positioning within a room can accommodate the temperature – and light – needs of most plants. Due to the lower intensity of sunlight after its transmission through windows, the majority of plants, including tropicals and temperate species used to growing in semi-shaded conditions, will tolerate, in fact require, as much light as possible, even full southern exposure, provided the area is well ventilated.

Moreover, no plant can contend with uncontrolled blasts of air at different temperatures, especially if those plants are living in shallow containers with limited soil to protect their root systems. In such situations, drafts can make their healthy existence a precarious one. Keeping them a safe distance back from windows and doors, especially those which are not double insulating panes and additional storm protection, goes a long way to maintaining necessary temperatures and preventing draft shock.

Some hardy outdoor plants can also be grown successfully indoors. Temperatures must register within the plant's natural range, and must work in tandem with light, which can be augmented by using fluorescent tubes or reflector panels of mirrored glass or foil.

If you live in an apartment, you can reproduce winter conditions by allowing your bonsai a stay in the refrigerator, if you have no alternative way to introduce a period of cold. You can induce fall's natural changes by simply reducing light conditions until pre-dormancy – with its color changes – then dormancy – marked by dropping of the leaves of deciduous plants – is encouraged.

Trees that spend summer outside should be brought indoors when fall approaches. They should be in place well before outdoor night-time temperatures drop below 50°F and before daytime temperatures also drop. Ideally, the indoor and outdoor temperatures should match, so the bonsai will not be sent into shock.

In an emergency such as unseasonally cold temperatures or loss of heat entirely, raising the humidity will help to counteract the ill-effects of the sudden change. There is potential danger in this, however, since if the humidity is raised too much and for too long a period, it could spur unseasonal or atypical plant growth, or cause the plant to become used to the new conditions, making a return to normal difficult. You must, therefore, take great care to limit the number of changes in growing conditions, and their frequency.

Practically speaking, a simple move of indoor bonsai from a warmer, lighter daytime exposure to a cooler, totally dark night-time holding area, imposes fewer demands than would building a special bonsai area inside. But it may create its own problems, if time and the constancy of your being home are variables.

Radiators, the saving grace for those who live in cold climates, are often the bane of the indoor bonsai's existence. Since radiators are often placed under windows, at the point of the greatest cold leakage, and the source of natural light for indoor plants is in the same area, temperature control can be a thorny problem. In fact, for indoor bonsai, the radiator definitely represents a mixed blessing as far as both temperature and humidity are concerned (see pp. 118–19).

A detail from the Satsuki opposite. The brilliant pink flowers are star shaped, and so closely packed on the branches that, in some areas, they almost obscure the foliage beneath. The azaleas are native to Japan, and among the most common flowering shrubs used in bonsai.

Air

One of the phenomena difficult to reproduce indoors is fresh air. For many bonsai, a hiatus outdoors during the summer, even if short-lived, is better than nothing. A temporary holding area can be as unpretentious as a picnic table on a terrace or fire escape. Since the bonsai are not used to the untempered elements of sun, wind, and rain, they will take a few weeks to become accustomed to the change. It is well to keep a sharp eye on them for signs of stress.

Most indoor bonsai growing in temperate to warm temperate regions can tolerate full exposure to the sun provided they are kept watered and are protected from drying winds. However, if there is any doubt as to the tree's tolerance of the full brunt of the sun and certainly if plants are small and in small containers, create a lath-type covering over the growing area to provide intermittent shade.

While outside, the circulation of air will help in the development of strong woody and leafy portions. It will also discourage the advance of disease and attack of pests. When normal air circulation becomes too strong, however, it can damage bonsai trees by knocking them over and even loosening them from their containers. This is often the point at which important branches can be injured or broken. To prevent it, the trees should be tied into their containers and then the whole tied to the display bench.

Before bonsai are once again brought indoors for the winter, take care to rid trees and soil of possible pests, to rid trees of disease, and to eliminate from their indoor growing area such noticeably opposing conditions that might send them into shock. For this reason, it is best to prepare the bonsai's winter home well before it will be needed, to allow you to bring indoor bonsai inside well before the weather starts to change.

Watering indoor bonsai

Watering indoor bonsai is much the same as watering outdoor bonsai, except that all the water must be supplied by you. There can be no refreshing night-time dew or sprinkle from a surprise afternoon shower. And, of course, no saturating rain. Instead, the bonsai has to depend on the reliability of its caretaker. It is your responsibility to provide the right amount of water.

The secret is in knowing the requirements and habits of the plants. A gardenia, for instance, would never survive the same watering regime as a cactus, and vice versa. One is a dramatic user of water, and needs humidity; the other is adapted to sharp drainage, sparse water, and low humidity.

What all indoor bonsai have in common is the need for water before their soil is bone dry, a condition betrayed in several different ways: the soil may be paler in color than usual; any moss on the surface may become dry and lackluster; when you put your finger into a corner of the pot, then withdraw it, no soil will stick to it; or, when you gently thump the pot on a solid surface, it sounds hollow.

The same principles apply to watering indoor bonsai as outdoor bonsai (see pp. 53–4), although indoor bonsai also need misting and steeping. It is wise to be cautious and mist indoor bonsai in the shade to prevent scorching and early enough in the day to allow the plant to dry before nightfall, so discouraging bacterial and fungal attack. Steeping, or immersion of the container and rootball in tepid water, is often used with indoor bonsai, too, but should be done only after the surface has first been watered to prevent moss and ground cover from being dislodged. It is particularly effective if the bonsai is wilting. It can be removed from the water once air bubbles have stopped rising to the surface, since this indicates that the soil has been completely moistened.

Water is most easily absorbed when tepid. In fact, warmish water taken directly from the tap is acceptable if it does not have too many added chemicals. If you have any doubts about your local tap water, have it tested and, if need be, find out how to correct its composition. Alternatively, keep a large, clean container of tap water near the collection and use the water after it has stood for a few days, after which time many of the volatile chemical additives will have dispersed.

Where tap water is unsuitable, some bonsaiists collect rainwater in containers, for exclusive use on their bonsai.

A nearby watering can fitted with a small, fine spray rosette, and a dipper or ladle, are invaluable aids.

You are more likely to have problems overwatering and underwatering when you are first learning to care for your

Jacaranda mimosifolia
Sharpleaf jacaranda
This plant started life in a tropical greenhouse, before being removed for training as a bonsai, and as such it is an excellent *subject for indoor bonsai. An informal upright, it is approximately forty years old, and featured in an exhibition of indoor bonsai at the Brooklyn Botanic Garden in 1976.*

bonsai. Inadvertent extremes are easy to reach, with the telltale signs rather hazy. It is important to remember that bonsai need less watering during the winter months since their growth is measurably slowed. Most bonsaiists determine the need for watering by the look and feel of the soil and the appearance of the tree and its leaves – all of which come with experience.

Humidity

Humidity is a major consideration with indoor bonsai and is all too often ignored or forgotten. The object is not to provide bonsai with high humidity necessarily but rather to provide the *correct* degree of humidity for the plants involved.

When the humidity level is too low, evaporation of water through the leaves exceeds the water taken in by the roots.

To avoid this problem before it starts, it is worth buying a hygrometer. This measures the relative humidity in the area and will show that, in a warm room, the relative humidity will be low since moisture evaporates in the heat. Moreover, it will tell you exactly how low it is, and give you concrete proof that, once you take steps to humidify the atmosphere, the situation is corrected. In any case, once central-heating systems take over during cold winter months, most indoor climates can use a healthy injection of humidity – it will have the side effects of making its inhabitants, human, animal and plant, even the wooden furniture, fitter.

A cool-vapor humidifier is the best kind to buy and is not expensive. Even more reasonable in terms of outlay would be to place bowls of water around the room in inconspicuous places, or resurrect the old-fashioned pans that hang from the coils of radiators. (Of course, that is only possible with old-fashioned coiled radiators, since modern

Punica granatum *Pomegranate Pomegranates are sun-lovers, and thrive indoors in full light where their bright scarlet tubular flowers can be appreciated. (Varieties with pink, yellow, and white flowers are also available.) They are also more likely to bear yellowish-red fruit indoors than out, since summer temperatures in temperate climates are rarely high enough for fruit production. This twisted-trunk style bonsai is from the Mansei-en Collection in Japan.*

apartment radiators do not provide the proper hanging places.)

Shallow, lipped plastic or metal trays filled with clean pebbles are very effective. Add water to the trays, to reach just below the surface of the pebbles. As the water evaporates upward, it increases the relative humidity of the immediate area. Since evaporation is a constant phenomenon, it is a good idea to check the water level every day, adding water as necessary. It is also a good idea to clean the trays regularly to remove any calcium and other deposits.

Misting is also an effective method of raising humidity, but its benefits are short-lived and can cause the bonsai more harm than good by making it endure a rapidly changing atmosphere. In no time the water vapor could be depleted, thereby demanding that the plants make yet another adjustment in their organic activity. A consistent situation would be far better, if necessary using the misting process only to augment an already existing and effective humidifying program.

Bonsai benefit every month or so from a shower. The bath is an ideal container, since it gives you enough room to spray the trunk as well as both the top and underside of leaves thoroughly. They can drip dry in the bath or in their usual location. By giving the trees a careful shower with tepid water, dust and foreign particles can be dislodged and rinsed away.

Fertilizer

The feeding of indoor bonsai plants does not differ appreciably from that of their outdoor relations. Their needs are the same, with nitrogen, phosphorus, and potash – the prime elemental food needs of all plants – at the top of the list.

Both organic and chemical fertilizers can provide these basic needs to bonsai, and are available as powders, liquids, and pellets. The fertilizer used depends upon the preference of the bonsaiist, which may be based on philosophy or convenience. Chemical products are available to the plant immediately; many organic fertilizers on the other hand are slower acting but have a much longer-term residual effect on the plant. Pellets of fertilizer are convenient and effective to use but have been found to give off an unpleasant odor, which is more noticeable indoors than outside.

Bonsai usually show signs that something is wrong in time for you to take action to correct the problem, even a problem as critical as nutrition. It could be that it was fed too soon after potting for instance; or that a root problem exists, one that is difficult to diagnose unless the roots are bared; then again, it could be that too much or too little fertilizer was used.

The business of too much or too little is easily determined by checking the amount and frequency of feeding against the manufacturer's recommendations. For safety sake, no matter what the recommended rate, feed bonsai a dilution – about half the recommended dose, rather than more. The normal once-a-month feeding during the spring and summer can be altered to small feedings at more frequent intervals . . . several small meals as opposed to one big feast every so often. Fertilizers designed specifically for bonsai can help in the determination of "what", "how much", and "how often" since they are geared for plants growing in small amounts of soil.

One practice which helps to prevent problems is to saturate the soil with water before feeding. Well-watered soil is less likely to retain generous amounts of fertilizer, reducing the likelihood of strong doses of fertilizer burning tender, young roots.

Timing, too, is a critical factor in the success of a feeding program. Generally, all plants require less food during the winter months when growth and metabolism have slowed.

Most plants will thrive with minimum feedings, perhaps one in mid- to late winter and no more until new spring growth sprouts. More frequent, small applications are in order until just before and during blooming, if the bonsai is flowering. After fruiting, if it produces fruit, feeding can continue.

Whether you choose to root prune or create new bonsai in the spring or fall, fertilizing is never appropriate immediately afterward. For about six to eight weeks, roots are recovering and just beginning to produce new growth. Until that process has begun, the roots are unable to absorb nutrients fully. If you find root damage on established bonsai during repotting, withhold fertilizer until the root system begins to regenerate.

As a rule of thumb, the younger the tree, the more fertilizer it can take. Also, stronger, faster growing trees will need more fertilizer than the slower growers. Neither, however, should be over-indulged during their period of winter dormancy.

Chapter 8
Bonsai Plants A-Z

This chapter presents a sample of effective, sturdy and "co-operative" bonsai plants.

Each variety is different in looks, needs, habit, and effect. If you familiarize yourself with these factors, through practice, you will be able to make valid judgments about which trees fit the conditions you can offer and the styles in which you want to train them.

It is important to remember, however, that there are no rules that cannot and have not been broken. Also, that which is generally true may prove untrue for you. For instance, within every climate zone there are microclimates. In fact, on a given piece of property there can be several microclimates, each differing enough from what is considered the norm, as to invalidate the prescribed procedures. Treat this basic table as a handy reference, not something to memorize but something which, after a while, you will develop a sixth sense about.

Notes: Temperature is only critical when dealing with indoor bonsai and non-native plants. The system used here was devised by the United States Department of Agriculture. Plants should thrive in the zone numbers given and in zones with higher numbers (and higher minimum winter temperatures). Average minimum winter temperatures for the climatic zones are:

①	Below −50°F	⑥	−10 to −0°F
②	−50 to −40°F	⑦	0 to 10°F
③	−40 to −30°F	⑧	10 to 20°F
④	−30 to −20°F	⑨	20 to 30°F
⑤	−20 to −10°F	⑩	30 to 40°F

Acer palmatum *Variegated Japanese maple*
Maples are classic bonsai subjects, popular in Japan and in the West, for both their spring and fall foliage. This twin-trunk bonsai is from the Ueda Collection, Japan.

ABIES (FIR)

- STYLES Formal upright, informal upright, slanting, cascade, literati, coiled, broom, split trunk, driftwood, root-over-rock, clinging-to-rock, twin trunk, clump, stump, raft, sinuous, forest, saikei.
- TEMPERATURE Differs according to variety.
- OUTDOOR
- HARDINESS RATING Hardy to zones 3–6, depending on variety.
- NON-FLOWERING
- EVERGREEN

A hardy evergreen conifer which prefers a cool growing season and unpolluted air. Keep in semi-shade. Available from bonsai specialists in seedling form or as seed.

- WHEN TO PRUNE Pinch the growing tips as often as needed during active growth period.
- WHEN TO REPOT Spring or fall.
- WHEN TO FERTILIZE Once a month in mid and late spring, early and mid fall.
- WHEN TO WATER Do not overwater, likes less rather than more. Mist needles.

SUITABLE VARIETIES

concolor (White, Silver, Colorado) Hardy to zone 4.
firma (Momi, Japanese) Hardy to zone 6.
homolepis (Nikko) Available from bonsai nurseries as seedlings and as seed. Hardy to zone 5.
koreana (Korean) Hardy to zone 5.
sachalinensis (Sakhalin) Hardy to zone 3.

ACER (MAPLE)

- STYLES Informal upright, slanting, cascade, semicascade, root-over-rock, twin trunk, clump, raft, sinuous, multiple trunk.
- TEMPERATURE Differs according to variety.
- OUTDOOR
- HARDINESS RATING Hardy to zones 3–6,

Detail of the leaves of Acer palmatum

depending on variety.
- FLOWERING
- DECIDUOUS

A most important group for the bonsaiist. Maples are hardy, beautiful, varied and found in northern temperate zones, with different varieties noted for different attributes such as interesting bark, beautiful leaves, unusual color. Requires semi-shade in summer, full sun the rest of the year, and protection from wind. Available in nurseries with more unusual forms found in bonsai nurseries in seedling and/or seed form.

- WHEN TO PRUNE Pinch in spring; main pruning in spring. When new shoots have developed three to five nodes, prune but leave one to two nodes. Trim leaves in late spring.
- WHEN TO REPOT Late winter/early spring.
- WHEN TO FERTILIZE Late winter/early spring.
- WHEN TO WATER Frequently as needed.

SUITABLE VARIETIES

buergerianum (Trident) Trim leaves in late spring or early summer. Brilliant reds and oranges in fall. Hardy to zone 6.
campestre (Hedge) Fall foliage bright yellow. Hardy to zone 5.
circinatum (Vine) Fall foliage red and

orange. Hardy to zone 6.
ginnala (Amur) Has yellowish-white flowers that hang in panicles and are fragrant. Scarlet foliage in fall. Hardy to zone 5.
palmatum (Japanese) A large category with many recognized varieties and cultivars. A diverse group both in the wild and in cultivation, it has leaves that range from green to red, purple and yellow, in addition to variegated cultivars with silver, pink, rose, white, cream, and green leaves. **A.p.** 'Dissectum' has deeply cut green leaves. Generally hardy to zone 5.
rubrum (Red, Scarlet, Swamp) Scarlet and orange fall foliage. Hardy to zone 3.

AZALEA

- STYLES Informal upright, slanting, cascade, semicascade, literati, root-over-rock, twin trunk, clump, stump, raft, forest.
- TEMPERATURE A wide range, differing according to variety.
- OUTDOOR/INDOOR
- HARDINESS RATING Differs according to variety.
- FLOWERING
- DECIDUOUS/EVERGREEN

Bonsaiists and gardeners often refer to azaleas as being in a genus of their own: they are not. They are members of the genus Rhododendron, flowering shrubs found all over the world except Africa and South America. The more commonly grown Rhododendrons are evergreen and have bell-shaped flowers.

Azaleas are more often deciduous and have funnel-shaped flowers. They appreciate protection from winter and summer sun, are happiest in humid climates and moderate temperatures, but require a fall in night-time temperatures to set buds. They span a whole palette of colors.

- WHEN TO PRUNE Following the shriveling of the flowers, prune back shoots to one or two nodes closest to the trunk.

- WHEN TO REPOT In late spring after blooming.
- WHEN TO FERTILIZE Several weeks after repotting.
- WHEN TO WATER Frequently, as needed.

SUITABLE VARIETIES

The following species are commonly referred to as azaleas. They are in the genus Rhododendron but are listed here for convenience. (See also *Rhododendron*.)

kaempferi (Torch) Semi-evergreen. Flowers are bright red, scarlet-rose, or pink to orange-red. Hardy to zone 6.

kiusianum (Kyushu) Semi-evergreen, with purple flowers. Repot every year after flowering. Needs semi-shade and frequent watering.

indicum (Satsuki) Evergreen. Repot every spring after flowering. Needs semi-shade, frequent watering, and cool to mild winters.

mucronatum (Ryukyu) Evergreen. Repot every year after flowering. Needs semi-shade, mild winters, and frequent watering.

obtusum (Kirishima, Hiryu) Evergreen, with rose-red to purple flowers. Hardy to zone 7.

serpyllifolium (Unzen, Wild thyme) Evergreen. Very small leaves, rosy-pink flowers. Repot every year after flowering. Hardy to zone 6.

BETULA (BIRCH)

- STYLES Informal upright, slanting, twin trunk, clump, raft, sinuous, multiple trunks.
- TEMPERATURE Usually to −25°F.
- OUTDOOR
- HARDINESS RATING Generally hardy to zone 2.
- FLOWERING

A rewarding group of trees readily available in nurseries, with pendent branches suited to colder climates. Needs full sun.

Detail of the flowers of Azalea indicum *Satsuki azalea.*

- WHEN TO PRUNE Prune shoots in late spring and on, leaving the one to two nodes closest to the trunk. Remove all suckers from base of tree.
- WHEN TO REPOT Before growth spurt in spring.
- WHEN TO FERTILIZE Spring and fall.
- WHEN TO WATER Frequently, but maintain dry atmosphere by keeping leaves unwatered.

SUITABLE VARIETIES

alleghaniensis (Yellow) Native to northeastern North America.

lenta (Black, Sweet, Cherry) A native of moist, cool woods.

papyrifera (Canoe, Paper, White) Native to the colder regions of North America. Oval leaves, white bark.

pendula (European). Leaves, which turn gold in fall, are heart- to diamond-shaped. There are numerous cultivars.

platyphylla Var. Japonica (Japanese white).

populifolia (Gray) Pale yellow leaves in fall.

BOUGAINVILLEA

- STYLES Informal upright, slanting, cascade, semicascade, exposed root, root-over-rock, twisted trunk.
- TEMPERATURE 45–75°F.
- OUTDOOR/INDOOR
- HARDINESS RATING Hardy only in zones 9 and 10. In colder areas, best kept in cool greenhouse or unheated sun-porch.
- FLOWERING
- EVERGREEN

A beautiful evergreen vining plant, available in a wide range of stunning colors.

- WHEN TO PRUNE Every year after flowering.
- WHEN TO REPOT Early spring.
- WHEN TO FERTILIZE A few weeks after repotting and again in early fall.
- WHEN TO WATER Frequently.

SUITABLE VARIETIES

buttiana 'Golden Glow' has bright yellow flowers fading to apricot; 'Louis Wathen' has orange flowers; and 'Mrs Butt' crimson.

glabra (Paper flower) Bright purple flowers.

peruviana Rosy-pink flowers.

BUXUS (BOXWOOD)

- STYLES Informal upright, slanting, semicascade, split trunk, root-over-rock, clinging-to-rock, twin trunk, clump, saikei.
- TEMPERATURE Differs according to variety.
- OUTDOOR
- HARDINESS RATING Hardy to zone 6.
- FLOWERING
- EVERGREEN

Boxwood has been grown in European, American and oriental gardens for centuries. Long-lived and slow growing, it thrives in full sun but will tolerate semi-shade. Keep boxwood cool but protected in winter. Available from nurseries.

- WHEN TO PRUNE Prune shoots back to one or two nodes as necessary.
- WHEN TO REPOT Spring, summer, or fall.
- WHEN TO FERTILIZE Early spring, fall.
- WHEN TO WATER Do not allow to dry out but do not overwater or growth will be too long.

SUITABLE VARIETIES

microphylla japonica (Japanese) Hardy to zone 6.
sempervirens (English, Common) Hardy to zone 6.

CAMELLIA

- STYLES Informal upright, slanting, cascade, semicascade, root-over-rock, twin trunk, clump, stump, raft, sinuous.
- TEMPERATURE Hardy to 10°F.
- OUTDOOR/INDOOR Happiest in temperate climate. Indoors needs cool nights that dip to 40–60°F. Outdoors in cool areas may need winter protection.
- HARDINESS RATING Hardy to zones 8–9.
- FLOWERING
- EVERGREEN

Camellias make particularly fine indoor bonsai. Favorable conditions are cool, not freezing, nights of 40–50°F during the flowering season. Camellias need partial shade and well-drained soil, yet plenty of light and water.

- WHEN TO PRUNE When the flowers have shriveled, but before new buds harden.
- WHEN TO REPOT Every year in late spring.
- WHEN TO FERTILIZE A few weeks after spring repotting and again in fall.
- WHEN TO WATER Frequently.

SUITABLE VARIETIES

japonica (Common) Flowers are red,

Detail of the leaves of Carpinus japonica *Japanese hornbeam.*

pink, or white and can be single or double. This species has larger leaves and stiffer branching than others. Hardy to zone 8.
reticulata Flowers are white, rose, or deep red and are frequently double. Smaller leafed and shade tolerant. Hardy to zone 9.

CARPINUS (HORNBEAM, IRONWOOD)

- STYLES Informal upright, slanting, cascade, semicascade, literati, root-over-rock, twin trunk, clump, forest, saikei.
- TEMPERATURE Differs according to variety.
- OUTDOOR
- HARDINESS RATING Hardy to zone 4.
- FLOWERING
- DECIDUOUS

Trees easy to train. Broad-leafed, with fragrant flowers, they prefer semi-shade during summer. Striking red and orange foliage color in fall. Hardy native in northern hemisphere and thrives in moist, woodsy soil.

- WHEN TO PRUNE Prune new shoots in spring before they open. As shoots develop three to five nodes and the branches are in a growth spurt, prune, leaving one or two nodes on the branch. Then, when the blossoms have shri-

veled but before the new buds harden, prune again. Major pruning in late winter.
- WHEN TO REPOT Early spring.
- WHEN TO FERTILIZE A few weeks after repotting in spring.
- WHEN TO WATER Mist and water frequently during summer, reducing water in winter.

SUITABLE VARIETIES

japonica (Japanese) Smooth pink-gray bark, strong-veined leaves.
laxiflora Loose-flowered.
tschonoskii (Yedoensis, Yeddo).

CEDRUS (CEDAR)

- STYLES Formal upright, split trunk, root-over-rock, twin trunk, clump, forest.
- TEMPERATURE 50–70°F; protect from elements.
- OUTDOOR
- HARDINESS RATING Hardy to zones 6–7.
- NON-FLOWERING
- EVERGREEN

An elegant conifer with clusters of rigid, needle-like leaves. Prefers full sun.

- WHEN TO PRUNE Pinch tips of new buds throughout the seasons. Prune in early spring or fall.
- WHEN TO REPOT Repot in spring before new growth expands.
- WHEN TO FERTILIZE Late winter and early spring; do not feed in mid and late summer; feed again in mid and late fall.
- WHEN TO WATER Water well in spring and summer, and reduce watering in fall.

SUITABLE VARIETIES

atlantica 'Glauca' (Blue Atlas) Needle tufts have a blue cast; branches are twisted. Hardy to zone 7.
deodara (Deodar, Indian) Gently contoured and easily trained, this must be checked regularly, since it often returns to

Chaenomeles japonica *Japanese flowering quince, in bloom.*

its original lines. Hardy to zone 7.
libani (Cedar of Lebanon) Slow-growing, hardy to zone 6.

CELTIS (HACKBERRY)

- STYLES Formal upright, informal upright, twin trunk, clump, forest.
- TEMPERATURE Moderate cold.
- OUTDOOR
- HARDINESS RATING Hardy to zone 7.
- FLOWERING
- DECIDUOUS

Found in temperate zones of the northern hemisphere.

- WHEN TO PRUNE Following the growth of several nodes, leave only the one or two nodes closest to the trunk.
- WHEN TO REPOT Early spring.
- WHEN TO FERTILIZE Very lightly a few weeks after repotting.
- WHEN TO WATER As needed, which will be frequently as the tree should be in full sun.

SUITABLE VARIETY

sinensis (Japanese) Characterized by dark-orange fruits, and a delicate twig structure. Hardy to the warmer parts of zone 7.

CHAENOMELES (FLOWERING QUINCE)

- STYLES Informal upright, slanting, cascade, semicascade, literati, coiled, exposed rock, root-over-rock, clinging-to-rock, twin trunk, clump, stump, raft, sinuous.
- TEMPERATURE Differs according to variety.
- OUTDOOR
- HARDINESS RATING Hardy to zone 5.
- FLOWERING
- DECIDUOUS/SEMI-EVERGREEN Depending on variety and zone.

Single- or double-flowering varieties are available in this old-fashioned favorite. In most varieties, flowers bloom before leaves unfurl. Mature specimens are known for their fruits, which are yellow and large but generally out of proportion for bonsai. In

addition, they sap the tree of energy, as does a prolific show of flowers. For this reason, you may want to prune off developing fruit and some of the flowers to preserve strength. This plant needs plentiful sunlight and water.

- WHEN TO PRUNE Pinch off all growth that sprouts from base of trunk. When new shoots develop five to seven nodes, prune to shape.
- WHEN TO REPOT Every three years in fall or late spring.
- WHEN TO FERTILIZE Spring before growth spurt.
- WHEN TO WATER Frequently.

SUITABLE VARIETIES

cathayensis Flowers range from pink to white. Hardy to zone 6.
japonica (Japanese) Grows in the wild in Japan. Salmon to orange flowers. Hardy to zone 5.
× *superba* 'Corallina' Red/orange flowers.

CHAMAECYPARIS (FALSE CYPRESS)

- STYLES Formal upright, informal upright, coiled, exposed root, root-over-rock, clinging-to-rock, twin trunk, clump, raft, forest.
- TEMPERATURE Differs according to variety.
- OUTDOOR
- HARDINESS RATING Hardy to zones 5–6.
- NON-FLOWERING
- EVERGREEN

A hardy conifer that requires semi-shade in summer. Available from general nurseries, and bonsai and specialist nurseries as seedlings.

- WHEN TO PRUNE Pinch during growth of new shoots in spring and early summer

Detail of the foliage of Chamaecyparis obtusa *Hinoki false cypress.*

and pinch tips of new buds any time when plant is in growth. Prune branches in early and mid spring, early and mid fall; major pruning in spring and fall.
- WHEN TO REPOT Spring, summer, fall.
- WHEN TO FERTILIZE Early spring.
- WHEN TO WATER Water well and mist foliage in summer.

SUITABLE VARIETIES

lawsoniana (Lawson cypress, Port Orford cedar) Hardy to zone 6; several suitable cultivars, including 'Nana' (Dwarf) and 'Nana Glauca', with a blue cast to branchlets.
obtusa 'Nana Gracilis' (Hinoki) Also used in full-size Japanese-style gardens. When immature, leaves bright yellow. Hardy to zone 5.
pisifera 'Snow' (Sawara) A strong, fast grower with green to yellow foliage. Rough to the touch. Likes moist, but not wet, lime-free soil and dislikes drying winds. New growth should be nipped or pulled off as it grows.

CORNUS (DOGWOOD)

- STYLES Informal upright, slanting, root-over-rock, twin trunk, clump.
- TEMPERATURE Differs according to variety.
- OUTDOOR
- HARDINESS RATING Hardy to zone 2.
- FLOWERING
- DECIDUOUS

Hardy and desirable, the dogwood is a tree with an interesting bark, and flowers in spring and berries in fall. It needs partial shade during summer, full sun the rest of the year.

- WHEN TO PRUNE After flowering and before new growth hardens. *Cornus* is among the group of trees known as bleeders; when cut prematurely in early spring, sap will run freely from the cut, debilitating the tree. Foliage beautifully colored in fall.
- WHEN TO REPOT Spring.
- WHEN TO FERTILIZE Spring/summer.
- WHEN TO WATER Frequently, as needed.

SUITABLE VARIETIES

florida (Flowering) Native to North America. Flowers showy due to prominent petal-like bracts. Red berries persist into winter. Hardy to zone 5.
kousa (Chinese) Blooms after *florida* and bracts persist for weeks. Branching is swirling and graceful, foliage bronze. Hardy to zone 5.

COTONEASTER

- STYLES Informal upright, slanting, cascade, semicascade, exposed root, root-over-rock, clinging-to-rock, twin trunk, clump, raft, sinuous.
- TEMPERATURE Differs according to variety.
- OUTDOOR
- HARDINESS RATING Hardy to zones 6–7.
- FLOWERING/BERRYING
- EVERGREEN/DECIDUOUS

White or pink flowers with small red to black fruit which persists throughout the fall and winter. Cotoneasters are ornamental and showy, and like well-drained soils. Grow in sun, shade and semi-shade, according to variety.

- WHEN TO PRUNE Prune when the new branches have three to five nodes, leaving one or two nodes.
- WHEN TO REPOT Any time during growing season.
- WHEN TO FERTILIZE Early spring.
- WHEN TO WATER Frequently.

SUITABLE VARIETIES

horizontalis (Rock spray) Broad-leafed evergreen with white to pink flowers. Hardy to zone 6.
microphyllus thymifolius Very compact; pink flowers, bright red fruits. Hardy to zone 7.

CRYPTOMERIA (JAPANESE CEDAR)

- STYLES Formal upright, twin trunk, clump, saikei.
- TEMPERATURE Not below 0°F.
- OUTDOOR
- HARDINESS RATING Hardy to zone 7.
- NON-FLOWERING
- EVERGREEN

A hardy evergreen with blue-green foliage, this likes semi-shade, moist soil, and warmth during winter. Grown as an ornamental in warmer temperate climates.

- WHEN TO PRUNE Pinch new growth before it opens in spring; prune heavy branches in spring.
- WHEN TO REPOT Repot in spring before new growth expands.
- WHEN TO FERTILIZE Mid spring and fall.
- WHEN TO WATER Frequently, from spring to fall. Mist foliage from spring to fall.

japonica (Common) Soft and shredding orange-brown bark. Hardy to zones 7–8.

CUPRESSUS (TRUE CYPRESS)

- STYLES Formal upright, root-over-rock, twin trunk, clump, forest.
- TEMPERATURE Differs according to variety.
- OUTDOOR/INDOOR
- HARDINESS RATING Hardy to zone 8.
- NON-FLOWERING
- EVERGREEN

A conifer, most varieties of which are hardy only in warmer climates without protection. Keep in semi-shade.

- WHEN TO PRUNE Pinch during new growth in spring and fall; prune branches in early and mid spring, early and mid fall; major pruning in spring and fall.
- WHEN TO REPOT Repot before new shoots open in spring or before new shoots harden in fall.
- WHEN TO FERTILIZE Late winter/early spring.
- WHEN TO WATER Frequently.

SUITABLE VARIETY

macrocarpa (Monterey) Interesting form and line, twisting contours.

EUGENIA

- STYLES Informal upright, slanted, forest.
- TEMPERATURES 45–68°F.
- INDOOR/OUTDOOR
- HARDINESS RATING Hardy to zones 9–10.
- FLOWERING
- EVERGREEN

A semi-tropical and vigorous grower. Careful pruning will help it keep its shape and encourage the leaves to reduce in size.

Its dark green leaves, glowing with a bronze cast when young, droop at the tips. The smooth, reddish bark is a good contrast to the small white flowers and dark red fruits.

SUITABLE VARIETY

uniflora (Surinam cherry) Fragrant white flowers and red and yellow fruits, which can be used in preserves and sherbets. Hardy to zone 10.

FAGUS (BEECH)

- STYLES Formal upright, informal upright, slanting, twin trunk, clump, raft, forest.
- TEMPERATURE Differs according to variety.
- OUTDOOR
- HARDINESS RATING Hardy to zones 4–6.
- FLOWERING
- DECIDUOUS

A magnificent genus with intriguing light-gray bark, beautiful buds, and good fall color. Leaves often remain on trees throughout the winter season. Distinctive markings on trunk are reminiscent of the creases in an elephant's hide. Prefers semi-shade in summer; full sun the rest of year.

- WHEN TO PRUNE When the new shoots have developed three to five nodes, prune but leave one to two nodes. Trim leaves once, in late spring.
- WHEN TO REPOT Spring.
- WHEN TO FERTILIZE A few weeks after spring potting.
- WHEN TO WATER Frequently.

SUITABLE VARIETIES

crenata (Japanese).
sylvatica (European) Hardy to zone 5. 'Pendula' has arching and pendulous branches; 'Purpurea' has purple leaves.

Details of the leaves and fruits of Cotoneaster microphyllus thymifolius *Cotoneaster.*

FORSYTHIA (GOLDEN BELLS)

- STYLES Informal upright, slanting, cascade, semicascade, root-over-rock, twin trunk, clump, raft, sinuous.
- TEMPERATURE 0°F according to variety.
- OUTDOOR
- HARDINESS RATING Hardy to zone 5.
- FLOWERING
- DECIDUOUS

Hardy harbinger of spring, forsythia blooms early with an abundance of yellow flowers that grace arching branches before the leaves appear. Disease-free, they are unfortunately often pruned to assume formal, unnatural shapes. Needs full sun.

- WHEN TO PRUNE After the flowers shrivel, but before the new buds harden, prune as desired, ie to desired shape.
- WHEN TO REPOT After flowering.
- WHEN TO FERTILIZE In early spring, before flowering.
- WHEN TO WATER When moderately dry.

SUITABLE VARIETIES

× *intermedia* Bright yellow spring flowers.
suspensa Native to China. Hardy to zone 5.

GARDENIA

- STYLES Informal upright, slanting, cascade, semicascade, clump.
- TEMPERATURE 60–75°F.
- INDOOR
- HARDINESS RATING Hardy to zone 9.
- FLOWERING
- EVERGREEN

Tender native of tropics and subtropics. Grown indoors or in greenhouses in temperate regions, the flowers are white or yellow and highly fragrant, backed by lusterous green leaves. Growing conditions must be kept consistent or buds and leaves will drop. Plant needs high humidity, good light, night temperatures of about 65°F and a good feeding program. Available from nurseries with a good selection of indoor plants.

- WHEN TO PRUNE Remove all flower buds that appear before early fall when buds can be allowed to set, flowering in winter.
- WHEN TO REPOT Late spring.
- WHEN TO FERTILIZE Early spring.
- WHEN TO WATER Very frequently. Mist leaves. Place on pebble tray.

SUITABLE VARIETIES

jasminoides (Cape gardenia) Large leaves with fragrant flowers which are often double; ***G.j. radicans*** (Dwarf) Smaller-leafed version of *jasminoides*.

GINKGO (MAIDENHAIR TREE)

- STYLES Informal upright, broom, twin trunk, clump, raft, sinuous.
- TEMPERATURE To 15°F.
- OUTDOOR
- HARDINESS RATING Hardy to zone 5.
- NON-FLOWERING
- DECIDUOUS

Hardy. An ancient species, grown as a

Detail of the leaves of Jacaranda mimosifolia *Sharpleaf jacaranda.*

street tree in temperate climates. Fall color is yellow. Form when leafless is beautiful. Select a male specimen: seeds of female trees emit an unattractive odor reminiscent of rancid butter.

- WHEN TO PRUNE After flowering, prune shoots, leaving the one to two nodes closest to the trunk.
- WHEN TO REPOT Late spring.
- WHEN TO FERTILIZE Late winter and spring.
- WHEN TO WATER As needed. Do not over-water.

SUITABLE VARIETY

biloba Hardy to zone 5.

HEDERA (IVY)

- STYLES Informal upright, slanted, cascade, semicascade, root-over-rock, twin trunk, clump.
- TEMPERATURE Differs according to variety.
- OUTDOOR
- HARDINESS RATING Generally hardy to zones 3–4.
- FLOWERING
- EVERGREEN

A hardy evergreen that needs rich soil and moisture, and prefers semi-shade.

Leaves are dark glossy green. The best source is your own garden, which may yield a woody section, rooted and ready for bonsaiing.

- WHEN TO PRUNE After new shoots have developed several nodes, cut back to the one or two nodes closest to the trunk.
- WHEN TO REPOT Spring.
- WHEN TO FERTILIZE Late winter, early spring.
- WHEN TO WATER Frequently.

SUITABLE VARIETIES

helix 'Hahnii' Bushy, with branching at tips.
rhombea (Japanese) Hardy to zone 8.

ILEX (HOLLY)

- STYLES Informal upright, slanted, cascade, semicascade, split turnk, root-over-rock, clinging-to-rock, twin trunk, clump, saikei.
- TEMPERATURE Differs according to variety.
- OUTDOOR
- HARDINESS RATING Hardy to zones 5–7, depending on variety (see below).
- FLOWERS Insignificant.
- EVERGREEN/DECIDUOUS Depends on variety. Generally, evergreens are hardy to zone 7 and deciduous varieties to zone 5.

A broad-leafed tree that berries, with the berries persisting through the winter, attracting birds of all kinds. Plants are either male or female, the female bearing the berries. For best pollination, male and female should be planted within 25 feet of each other. Most nurseries carry a selection of *Ilex*, with rarer varieties available at bonsai and specialist nurseries in both seedling and seed form.

- WHEN TO PRUNE After flowering, when new shoots have sprouted with several nodes, cut back to the one or two nodes closest to the trunk.

- WHEN TO REPOT Early spring.
- WHEN TO FERTILIZE Several weeks after repotting.
- WHEN TO WATER Frequently.

SUITABLE VARIETIES

crenata (Japanese, Box-leafed) Evergreen. Flowers are white, berries are black. Hardy to zone 6.

pernyi (Perny) Evergreen. Flowers yellow, fruit red. Hardy to zone 6.

serrata (Japanese winterberry) Deciduous. Flowers lavender to white, fruit is red. Hardy to zone 5.

vomitoria (Yaupon) Evergreen, with berries that can be either red or yellow. Hardy to zone 7.

JACARANDA (GREEN EBONY)

- STYLES Informal upright, cascade, semicascade, clump.
- TEMPERATURE Tropical and semi-tropical.
- OUTDOOR/INDOOR Grown in greenhouses in cooler climates.
- HARDINESS RATING Hardy to zone 9.
- FLOWERING
- EVERGREEN

An impressive shrub native to the tropical Americas, with blooms that range from blue to violet, and, rarely, white or pink. Flowers are showy; grown indoors in colder areas.

- WHEN TO PRUNE Before repotting in early spring or in fall.
- WHEN TO REPOT Early spring, fall.
- WHEN TO FERTILIZE Several weeks after repotting.
- WHEN TO WATER Frequently. Keep soil moist but not soaking. Keep drier during winter.

SUITABLE VARIETIES

caerulea Flowers white, blue, or lilac.
mimosifolia Blue flowers.

Detail of the foliage of Juniperus chinensis *Chinese juniper.*

JASMINUM (TRUE JASMINE)

- STYLES Informal upright, slanted, cascade, semicascade, exposed root, root-over-rock, clinging-to-rock, twin trunk, clump, raft, sinuous.
- TEMPERATURE Differs according to variety.
- OUTDOOR/INDOOR
- HARDINESS RATING Hardy to zone 6.
- FLOWERING
- DECIDUOUS/SEMI-DECIDUOUS

Hardy to a degree, with the less hardy varieties thriving in greenhouse conditions, jasmines are easy to care for.

- WHEN TO PRUNE When the flowers have shriveled but before the new buds have hardened. Prune off any new shoots emanating from base of tree.
- WHEN TO REPOT Early spring.
- WHEN TO FERTILIZE Several weeks after repotting.
- WHEN TO WATER Frequently.

SUITABLE VARIETIES

floridum (Showy) Yellow flowers. Hardy to zone 7.

nudiflorum (Winter) Fragrant. Showy yellow flowers in early spring. Hardy to zone 6.

× *stephanense* Pink flowers. Fragrant.

JUNIPERUS (JUNIPER)

- STYLES Cascade, semicascade, literati, coiled, driftwood, windswept, exposed root, root-over-rock, clinging-to-rock, twin trunk, clump, raft, sinuous, natural grouping.
- TEMPERATURE Differs according to variety.
- OUTDOOR
- HARDINESS RATING Hardy to zones 3–6, depending on variety.
- NON-FLOWERING
- EVERGREEN

Hardy conifers, with many varieties that are easy to grow, prune, and train. Rewarding, with responsive, fairly rapid growth. Available at nurseries in many varieties. Those not found can be ordered from bonsai specialists in seedling form. One caution – wear gloves when working with junipers, for the prick of the needles can produce an allergic reaction that causes itchy red bumps.

- WHEN TO PRUNE Pinch out the tips of new buds any time during the growth period. Major pruning in spring or fall, but not in summer.
- WHEN TO REPOT Repot any time except winter, especially in early/mid spring before new shoots open.
- WHEN TO FERTILIZE Early spring.
- WHEN TO WATER Thoroughly, but allow to dry out between waterings.

SUITABLE VARIETIES

chinensis (Chinese) Native to China, Mongolia, and Japan. Hardy to zone 4. Cultivated varieties include *procumbens* (Japanese), a low grower with short green needles which sometimes shows a slight blue cast; 'Nana', the dwarf form of *J. chinensis*, which retains the graceful habit of the parent; and *J.c.* 'Sargentii' (Sargent), a dense plant with drooping branches.

conferta (Shore).

horizontalis (Creeping) Long, trailing branches with blue-green cast. Hardy to zone 3.

Detail of the foliage of Juniperus rigida
Needle juniper.

rigida (Temple, Needle) Spreading habit. Naturally drooping branches. Hardy to zone 6 but in need of winter protection.
sabina horizontalis (Creeping, Spreading) Hardy to zone 3.
scopulorum (Rocky Mountain, Colorado red cedar) Hardy to zone 4.

LARIX (LARCH)

- STYLES Formal upright, informal upright, slanting, split trunk, driftwood, root-over-rock, clinging-to-rock, twin trunk, clump, forest.
- TEMPERATURE Differs according to variety.
- OUTDOOR
- HARDINESS RATING Hardy to zones 3–5 depending on variety.
- NON-FLOWERING
- DECIDUOUS

This needled, coniferous tree is deciduous. The foliage of the larch is short and fine. Cones are small and useful for floral arrangements and holiday decorations. Prefers semi-shade in summer, full sun the rest of the year.

- WHEN TO PRUNE Pinch tips of new buds during growth period; prune subbranches in mid spring, main branches in mid winter.

- WHEN TO REPOT Early to mid spring.
- WHEN TO FERTILIZE Spring and fall.
- WHEN TO WATER Requires moisture without constant puddling.

SUITABLE VARIETY

kaempferi (Japanese) Bluish-green needles. Hardy to zone 5.

LEPTOSPERMUM (NEW ZEALAND TEA, MANUKA)

- STYLES Informal upright, slanting, split trunk, twin trunk, clump, stump.
- TEMPERATURE Requires indoor temperatures of 55–60°F.
- OUTDOOR/INDOOR Outdoor in warm climates; greenhouse in colder climates.
- HARDINESS RATING Hardy to zone 9.
- FLOWERING
- EVERGREEN

Informal shrubs or small trees that are native to Australia, Malaysia, and New Zealand.

- WHEN TO PRUNE After flowering.
- WHEN TO REPOT Early spring.
- WHEN TO FERTILIZE Several weeks after repotting and then once a month thereafter.
- WHEN TO WATER Frequently, as needed. Mist leaves.

SUITABLE VARIETY

scoparium (New Zealand tea) A bushy species, this has five-petalled pink or white flowers. Hardy to zone 9.

LESPEDEZA (BUSH CLOVER)

- STYLES Informal upright, slanting, cascade, semicascade, root-over-rock, clinging-to-rock, twin trunk, clump.
- TEMPERATURE −10°F.
- OUTDOOR
- HARDINESS RATING Hardy to zone 5.
- FLOWERING
- DECIDUOUS

A deciduous shrub, with arching branches bearing the clover-shaped leaves, and flowers.

- WHEN TO PRUNE Cut back branches in late fall, trim shoots after flowers fall from tree.
- WHEN TO REPOT Any time, with spring and fall slightly better than summer or winter.
- WHEN TO FERTILIZE Early spring.
- WHEN TO WATER Frequently.

SUITABLE VARIETIES

cyrtobotrya Flowers are purplish-rose.
japonica Flowers are white.

MALUS (CRABAPPLE, APPLE)

- STYLES Informal upright, slanting, cascade, semicascade, root-over-rock, twin trunk, stump.
- TEMPERATURE Differs according to variety.
- OUTDOOR
- HARDINESS RATING Hardy to zones 2–8, depending on variety.
- FLOWERING
- DECIDUOUS

Grown for fruit and flowers, these are natives of cool temperate areas. The hybrids developed are habitués of the same climates, with the oriental varieties sporting the smallest, showiest flowers and fruit. The crabapples are important in bonsai, but special attention must be paid to potential insect damage, including sucking injuries from aphids. If present, remove with a strong blast of water from hose. Found around old houses, and in old gardens, otherwise easily located in nurseries, with rarer varieties found in bonsai or specialist nurseries.

- WHEN TO PRUNE Prune after flowers have shriveled but before new buds harden.
- WHEN TO REPOT Repot every year in early spring, after flowering, or in early fall.
- WHEN TO FERTILIZE Every week during spring, summer and early fall with either a diluted mixture of a complete fertilizer or, preferably, a diluted application of manure tea.
- WHEN TO WATER Frequently.

SUITABLE VARIETIES

baccata (Siberian) Flowers white, fruit bright red. Hardy to zone 2. **var. mandshurica** Likes full sun and thorough watering, manure tea feeding; white flowers. Hardy to zone 2.
floribunda (Japanese, Showy) Flowers start as rose, then pale to pink, fruit is yellow; hardy to zone 5.
halliana (Hall's crabapple) Bright rose flowers, fruit is a shade of purple; hardy to zone 6.
× **micromalus** (Kaido, Dwarf) Flowers are deep pink, fruit is yellow; hardy to zone 5.
pumila Hardy to zone 4.
sargentii (Sargent, Dwarf) Flowers are white, fruit is red. Hardy to zone 2.
sieboldii (Toringo) Flowers are bright pink fading to white, fruit is red to yellowish-brown. Hardy to zone 2.
transitoria (Cut-leaf) The most delicate listed, with white flowers, and bright red fruit.

MISCANTHUS (WATER GRASS)

- STYLES Clinging-to-rock, planting of herbs, grasses.

- TEMPERATURE 0°F.
- OUTDOOR
- HARDINESS RATING Hardy to zone 5.
- FLOWERING
- PERENNIAL

A large genus of ornamental grasses that accompany bonsai. Some are as tall as 6 feet in their natural state, some as short as 3 feet. Grown for their silky panicles. Need shade during summer and warmth during winter. If happy, will self-sow.

- WHEN TO PRUNE Pinch shoots when they first appear.
- WHEN TO REPOT Every two years.
- WHEN TO FERTILIZE Early spring when shoots appear.
- WHEN TO WATER Frequently.

SUITABLE VARIETIES

sacchariflorus (Amur silver grass)
sinensis 'Yaku Jima' A miniature form.

OLEA (OLIVE)

- STYLES Formal upright, informal upright, cascade, semicascade, clump, forest.
- TEMPERATURE 35–60°F.
- OUTDOOR/INDOOR
- HARDINESS RATING Hardy to zone 9.
- FLOWERING
- EVERGREEN

An easy plant for the beginner, grown for foliage as well as fruit. Olives develop after several weeks of the following temperature regime: 35°F at night to 60°F during the day. The tree features small leaves with a gray cast and a trunk that contorts in maturity. Found on farmland, in orchards, and in specialist nurseries.

- WHEN TO PRUNE As needed, any time of year.
- WHEN TO REPOT Every two or three years.

Details of the flowers and leaves of Lespedeza cyrtobotrya *Bush clover.*

- WHEN TO FERTILIZE Every month during growing season.
- WHEN TO WATER When watering, water thoroughly, but keep it on the dry side.

SUITABLE VARIETY

europaea (Common) Hardy to zone 9.

PARTHENOCISSUS (BOSTON OR JAPANESE IVY, WOODBINE)

- STYLES Informal upright, slanting, cascade, semicascade, root-over-rock, twin trunk, clump.
- TEMPERATURE 0°F or above.
- OUTDOOR
- HARDINESS RATING Hardy to zone 5.
- FLOWERING
- DECIDUOUS

A hardy, broad-leafed vine, deciduous in all climates. Large, shiny leaves of deep green, and dark-blue fruit. Needs semi-shade in summer, full sun the rest of the year. Good fall color and good form when leafless.

- WHEN TO PRUNE Following its fruiting, but before the new buds have hardened, prune the ivy back to the desired position.
- WHEN TO REPOT Early spring.

- WHEN TO FERTILIZE Early spring and fall.
- WHEN TO WATER Mist leaves in summer.

tricuspidata (Japanese) Hardy to zone 5.

PICEA (SPRUCE)

- STYLES Formal upright, informal upright, slanting, cascade, semicascade, literati, coiled, driftwood, root-over-rock, clinging-to-rock, twin trunk, clump raft, sinuous, forest.
- TEMPERATURE Differs according to variety.
- OUTDOOR
- HARDINESS RATING Generally hardy to zone 6.
- NON-FLOWERING
- EVERGREEN

A popular, hardy conifer. Most varieties like full sun.

- WHEN TO PRUNE Pinch new growth a couple of times in spring, removing new shoots before they harden. Leave about four to five clusters of needles. Major pruning in early fall and, every couple of years, prune drastically, leaving about five needle clusters closest to trunk. Never remove all needles.
- WHEN TO REPOT Repot in spring before new growth expands or early fall. Protect from full sun for a few weeks after repotting.
- WHEN TO FERTILIZE Late winter/early spring and in fall.
- WHEN TO WATER Frequently but allow to dry out between waterings. Mist in spring, summer, fall.

SUITABLE VARIETIES

abies 'Maxwellii' (Norway) A naturally dwarf form, hardy to zone 3.
engelmannii (Blue Englemann) Native to the western part of North America. Hardy to zone 3.
glauca (White) Hardy to zone 3.

Detail of the foliage of Picea jezoensis *Silver spruce.*

glehnii (Sakhalin, Common Ezo or Edo, Yedo or Yesso spruce)
jezoensis (Yeddo, Silver, Hondo) Likes semi-shade. Hardy to zone 5.
orientalis (Oriental) Hardy to zone 5.
pungens (Colorado) Hardy to zone 3.
torana (Tiger-tail) Hardy to zone 6.

PIERIS (ANDROMEDA)

- STYLES Informal upright, slanting, semicascade, cascade, root-over-rock, twin trunk, clump.
- TEMPERATURE Differs according to variety.
- OUTDOOR
- HARDINESS RATING Hardy to zones 1–7, depending on variety.
- FLOWERING
- EVERGREEN

A genus of naturally compact, ornamental shrubs. Most varieties are hardy and thrive in semi-shade. Plant is best served if buds are protected during winter, and from spring frosts. Available at almost all nurseries, or dig up an old shrub in a foundation planting and bonsai it!

- WHEN TO PRUNE Prune after the flowers shrivel but before new buds harden toward the end of summer.
- WHEN TO REPOT Early spring.

- WHEN TO FERTILIZE Early spring.
- WHEN TO WATER Moderately.

SUITABLE VARIETIES

formosa (Chinese) Hardy to zones 6–7.
japonica 'Variegata' (Lily-of-the-valley bush) Hardy to zone 6; has white leaf margins as contrast. 'Nana' is a naturally dwarf grower, hardy to zone 1.

PINUS (PINE)

- STYLES Formal upright, informal upright, slanting, cascade, semicascade, literati, driftwood, exposed root, root-over-rock, clinging-to-rock, twin trunk, clump, stump, forest.
- TEMPERATURE Differs according to variety.
- OUTDOOR
- HARDINESS RATING Hardy to zones 3–8.
- NON-FLOWERING
- EVERGREEN

Pines have often been referred to as the kings of trees. In fact, in bonsai lore the Japanese black pine is referred to as the warrior, the samurai. It is logical, then, that the pine has come to stand for strength, with its sturdy architecture and branching habits. And, in a seeming contradiction, also to stand for beauty, with its lusterous green needles and artistry. Fortunately pines are diverse enough to be found thriving in a variety of growing conditions. This gives the bonsai lover the opportunity to select the correct variety for the conditions that exist. Pines make dramatic bonsai, but naturally some species are easier to grow than others. Most are available in nurseries, and the more unusual can be ordered from specialist nurseries in seedling or seed form. Like full sun. Be careful not to overwater, and protect from wind and salt air.

- WHEN TO PRUNE Pinch new growth in spring after the first rush of growth has taken place. For more compact growth, take bundle of candles between fingers

Pinus parviflora *Japanese white pine from the Ueda Collection, Japan.*

muricata (Bishop) Hardy to zone 8.
parviflora (Japanese white, Five-needle). Every year or two, remove new needles before they harden. Tolerates wind. Likes full sun and rather dry conditions. Hardy to zone 6. Often called **P. pentaphylla** in Japanese literature.
pumila (Creeping five-needle, Dwarf stone) Tolerates sun and wind. Hardy to zone 4.
rigida (Pitch) Thrives on poor soil. Hardy to zone 5.
sylvestris (Scots) Has blue-green needles, and flaking bark. One of the hardiest pines, hardy to zone 3.
thunbergii (Japanese black, Nishiki) Full sun, likes to be on the dry side, tolerates wind and salt air; do not bruise bark on trunk. Hardy to zone 5.

and twist or pinch off at least half their length. If drastic pruning is needed, remove the new candles entirely. If needles become too long, trim them, then reduce the quantity of needles on each branch. Prune several times each spring. In early spring, remove undesirable branches that clutter the inside of the tree structure and small branches that will serve no visual or structural function in the future. In summer, if needles are still too long, trim them to one-third their length. Then fertilize, and new needles will emerge to restore foliage to the proper proportions. In early fall, every few years, prune each branch tip back so that about five to six needle clusters remain closest to the trunk.

- WHEN TO REPOT Repot once every three years close to the end of fall or in early/mid spring in cold climates; in warmer climates, repot earlier, but before new needles open.
- WHEN TO FERTILIZE Don't fertilize until all new growth is fully developed. When necessary, feed in early to mid summer, after new growth has hardened, with diluted manure tea or weak commercial fertilizer.
- WHEN TO WATER In spring, when actively growing, water sparingly rather than frequently, once a day. Do not overwater. On hot days, water twice a day, or as often as needed.

SUITABLE VARIETIES

albicaulis (Whitebark) Native to the American Pacific Northwest. Hardy to zone 4.
aristata (Bristlecone) Slow grower. Hardy to zone 6.
contorta (Shore) Hardy to zone 7.
densiflora (Japanese red) The most delicate of the pines. Likes dry conditions and needs good protection from harsh winters. Hardy to zone 5.
koraiensis (Korean) Every two to three years, remove new needles. Tolerates wind but needs protection. Hardy to zone 3.
mugo (Mountain, Swiss mountain) Hardy to zone 3.

PRUNUS (FLOWERING ALMOND)

- STYLES Informal upright, slanting, cascade, semicascade, literati, coiled, split trunk, driftwood, root-over-rock, clinging-to-rock, twin trunk, clump, raft, forest, saikei.
- TEMPERATURE 40–60°F.
- OUTDOOR
- HARDINESS RATING Hardy to zones 3–8, depending on the variety.
- FLOWERING
- DECIDUOUS

Hardy shrub, well branched with interesting foliage in fall. Keep cool, preferably in a greenhouse.

- WHEN TO PRUNE After flowering in early spring, and fall.
- WHEN TO REPOT Early spring and fall.
- WHEN TO FERTILIZE Early spring before flowering, and fall.
- WHEN TO WATER Frequently, as needed.

Pinus thunbergii *Japanese black pine from the Oguchi Collection, Japan.*

SUITABLE VARIETIES

---

dulcis Double flowers in a spectrum of whites and pinks. Hardy to zone 7.

glandulosa (Flowering) Flowers in whites and pinks, fruits are dark red. Hardy to zone 4.

triloba (Double flowering) Double white or pink flowers, red fruits. Hardy to zone 3.

PRUNUS (FLOWERING APRICOT)

- STYLES Informal upright, slanting, cascade, semicascade, twin trunk, clump.
- TEMPERATURE Warm, with cooler nights to encourage flowering and fruiting.
- OUTDOOR
- HARDINESS RATING Hardy to zone 7.
- FLOWERING
- DECIDUOUS

Cultivated from about 2000 BC in China, this is a classic bonsai subject. Flowers are pink, fruits red – later flowers are white to dark red, fruits yellow to dark green. Likes full sun, tempered with some shade during the hottest part of the summer. Try to avoid over-blooming, which can be harmful.

- WHEN TO PRUNE Allow new shoots to develop until late summer, when each new shoot can be pruned back, leaving one to two nodes or more, as desired.
- WHEN TO REPOT Early spring.
- WHEN TO FERTILIZE Appreciates manure tea during growing season.
- WHEN TO WATER Frequently, as needed.

SUITABLE VARIETY

---

mume (Japanese apricot) The famed "plum" of the Orient. White to dark-red flowers in winter with yellow to green fruits. Hardy to zone 7.

PRUNUS (FLOWERING CHERRY)

- STYLES Informal upright, slanting, cascade, semicascade, twin trunk, clump, raft, sinuous, two and three tree groups.
- TEMPERATURE Hardy to 0°F, except for *P. japonica*.
- OUTDOOR
- HARDINESS RATING Hardy to zones 3–8, depending on variety.
- FLOWERING
- DECIDUOUS

An important symbol of Japan, with many varieties appropriate for bonsai. Found in old farmyards and nurseries and, for rarer varieties, in bonsai nurseries. Prefers semi-shade in summer and full sun the rest of the year. Unfortunately, all varieties are intolerant of air pollution.

- WHEN TO PRUNE When the blossoms have shriveled, but before new buds harden.
- WHEN TO REPOT Early spring; following blooming time; fall.
- WHEN TO FERTILIZE During growing, season, water with manure tea.
- WHEN TO WATER Frequently, especially in summer.

SUITABLE VARIETIES

---

campanulata (Formosa, Taiwan) Early flowers of deep rose red. Fruits are red. Hardy to zone 8.

incisa (Fuji) Flowers are red or pink, fruits are purple-black, and foliage turns orange in fall. Hardy to zone 6.

japonica (Japanese single bush cherry, Japanese plum) Flowers range from pink to white, has wine-red edible fruits. This is the most tender variety, requiring slightly warmer climatic conditions than others. Hardy to zone 4.

pseudocerasus Flowers are white and fragrant. Hardy to zone 6.

serrulata (Oriental, or Japanese flowering cherry) Flowers are white, fruits are black. Several cultivars are also suitable for bonsai, including 'Kanzan'.

subhirtella (Higan, Rosebud) Off-white to pink flowers, black fruit. Hardy to zone 6. ***P.s.*** 'Pendula' (Weeping) has weeping growth. The small branches are contorted and pendulous.

tomentosa (Korean bush-cherry, Nanking cherry) White flowers, red berries. Very winter hardy, to zone 3.

PRUNUS (FLOWERING PEACH)

- STYLES Informal upright, slanted, cascade, semicascade, twin trunk, clump.
- TEMPERATURE Differs according to variety.
- OUTDOOR
- HARDINESS RATING Hardy to zone 7.
- FLOWERING
- DECIDUOUS

Tree will thrive in full sun throughout the summer if watering is frequent and thorough enough. Available in most nurseries and through bonsai nurseries.

- WHEN TO PRUNE Following the shriveling of the flowers, but before the new buds harden, prune carefully.
- WHEN TO REPOT Early spring, after flowering, early fall.
- WHEN TO FERTILIZE After flowering in spring, and fall.
- WHEN TO WATER Frequently.

SUITABLE VARIETIES

dulcis White to pink flowers; fruits are inedible. Hardy to zone 7.

PRUNUS (FLOWERING PLUM)

- STYLES Informal upright, slanting, cascade, semicascade, twin trunk, clump.
- TEMPERATURE Differs according to variety.
- OUTDOOR

Detail of the buds of **Prunus subhirtella** *Higan flowering cherry.*

- HARDINESS RATING Hardy to zone 8.
- FLOWERING
- DECIDUOUS

Another species important to bonsai, this requires semi-shade in summer, full sun the rest of the year.

- WHEN TO PRUNE When the blossoms have shriveled, but before the buds have hardened, prune back as desired.
- WHEN TO REPOT Every year in early spring.
- WHEN TO FERTILIZE After flowering in spring and fall.
- WHEN TO WATER Frequently.

SUITABLE VARIETIES

cerasifera (Myrobalan, Cherry) Vigorous with beautiful, small white blossoms. 'Atropurpurea' is a purple-leafed variety, with variations that go from a coppery-red to almost black.

salicina (Japanese) White flowers, and red or yellow fruits. Hardy to zone 8.

PUNICA (POMEGRANATE)

- STYLES Informal upright, slanting, cascade, semicascade, literati, twin trunk, clump, raft, sinuous, two and three tree grouping, saikei.
- TEMPERATURE 45–68°F.
- INDOOR
- HARDINESS RATING Hardy to zone 9.
- FLOWERING
- DECIDUOUS

Easy to grow but needs good winter protection, though it is hardy outdoors in temperatures that do not fall below 40°F. Used frequently as indoor bonsai material. Wonderful trunk, delicate leaves, red fruits, and yellow foliage in fall. Flowers are orangy-red. Needs semi-shade in summer and full sun the rest of the year.

- WHEN TO PRUNE In early spring or late fall, prune back the shoots leaving only one or two nodes. Repeat during the summer. Always remove the suckers that spring up from the base of the trunk.
- WHEN TO REPOT Following the opening of the new leaves in spring.
- WHEN TO FERTILIZE Early spring, fall.
- WHEN TO WATER Frequently.

SUITABLE VARIETY

granatum 'Nana' (Dwarf) Bears fruit early.

PYRACANTHA (FIRETHORN)

- STYLES Informal upright, slanting, cascade, semicascade, root-over-rock, clinging-to-rock, twin trunk, clump, saikei.
- TEMPERATURE 0°F and above.
- OUTDOOR
- HARDINESS RATING Hardy to zone 7.
- FLOWERING/BERRYING
- EVERGREEN

Detail of the leaves of Sequoia sempervirens *Coast redwood.*

An easy shrub to grow, but be careful of the thorns, for which it is appropriately named. Several varieties, most of which have red or orange berries in fall, though some have yellow berries. Check local nurseries, then bonsai and specialist nurseries for the more unusual types. Needs full sun.

- WHEN TO PRUNE When the flowers have shriveled, but before the new buds have hardened. Well-planned pruning encourages heavier flowering and fruiting.
- WHEN TO REPOT Spring.
- WHEN TO FERTILIZE Early spring and fall.
- WHEN TO WATER Frequently.

SUITABLE VARIETIES

angustifolia Orangy-red berries. Hardy to zone 7.

coccinea Small, white flowers, and red fruit. Hardy to zone 7.

fortuneana Hardy to zone 7.

QUERCUS (OAK)

- STYLES Informal upright, slanting, semicascade, twin trunk, clump.
- TEMPERATURE Differs according to variety.
- OUTDOOR

- HARDINESS RATING Hardy to zone 5.
- FLOWERS INSIGNIFICANT
- DECIDUOUS

Hardy. An added bonus is the fall color of red, orange, yellow, mahogany. Form when leafless is beautiful. Needs full sun all year except winter, when it thrives in semi-shade. Available in nurseries or from bonsai specialists in both seedling and seed form.

- WHEN TO PRUNE Pinch in summer; major pruning in late spring/early summer.
- WHEN TO REPOT Early spring.
- WHEN TO FERTILIZE Spring.
- WHEN TO WATER Moderately.

SUITABLE VARIETIES

agrifolia (California live) Hardy to zone 9.

dentata (Daimyo) Hardy to zone 6.

glandulifera (Serrata, Japanese, Konara). Large leaves. Hardy to zone 6.

marilandica (Blackjack) Hardy to zone 6.

myrsinifolia (Bamboo-leaved) Hardy to zone 8.

palustris (Pin, Spanish) Hardy to zone 5.

suber (Cork) Famed for the thick bark which provides cork used around the world. Hardy to zone 8.

RHODODENDRON

- STYLES Informal upright, slanting, cascade, semicascade, root-over-rock, clinging-to-rock, twin trunk, raft, forest.
- TEMPERATURE Differs according to variety.
- OUTDOOR
- HARDINESS RATING Differs according to variety.
- FLOWERING
- DECIDUOUS

A hardy shrub that flowers magnificently in an incredible array of colors. Keep in semi-shade.

- WHEN TO PRUNE Late winter/early spring as needed.
- WHEN TO REPOT Every three years in late winter/early spring.
- WHEN TO FERTILIZE Late winter/early spring and fall.
- WHEN TO WATER Water frequently: appreciates dampness.

SUITABLE VARIETIES

degronianum Soft pink flowers. Hardy to zone 7.

fastigiatum (Chinese) Light purple. Hardy to zone 7.

flavidum (Amberbloom) Yellow flowers. Hardy to zone 6.

impeditum (Cloudland) Purplish-blue and fragrant flowers. Hardy to zone 6.

metternichii (Leatherleaf) Rose with deeper rose spots. Hardy to zone 6.

myrtifolium (Myrtle) Lilac pink flowers. Hardy to zone 6.

racemosum (Mayflower) White, pink, or rose flowers. Hardy to zone 6.

rupicola (Cliffplum) Flowers are dark purple-crimson. Hardy to zone 7.

williamsianum Pale rose flowers. Hardy to zone 7.

(See also **Azalea**)

ROSMARINUS (ROSEMARY)

- STYLES Informal upright, slanting, cascade, semicascade, root-over-rock.
- TEMPERATURE 45°F.
- OUTDOOR/INDOOR
- HARDINESS RATING Hardy to zone 8.
- FLOWERING
- EVERGREEN

A herb found in almost all herb gardens and used by chefs around the world. Small leaves, a trunk that twists naturally, and bark that is visually interesting are all factors in making this such a good bonsai subject. Hardy only in milder climates, it can be brought indoors for the colder months as long as it gets as much light as possible and cool temperatures at night.

Do not let it dry out. Available at any local nursery.

- WHEN TO PRUNE Anytime.
- WHEN TO REPOT Early spring.
- WHEN TO FERTILIZE Early spring, fall.
- WHEN TO WATER Frequently. Mist leaves.

SUITABLE VARIETY

officinalis (Common) Tiny blue, white, or pink flowers in spring. Hardy to zone 9. In immediately colder zones, it might make it through the winter with ample protection. "Prostratus" (Dwarf) has blue flowers and fine leaves.

SALIX (WILLOW)

- STYLES Informal upright, slanting, cascade, semicascade, root-over-rock, clinging-to-rock, twin trunk.
- TEMPERATURE A wide range, differing according to variety.
- OUTDOOR
- HARDINESS RATING Best in zones 5–10, depending on variety.
- FLOWERS INSIGNIFICANT
- DECIDUOUS

Easy, hardy tree with a dramatic leafy look and a natural weeping tendency. A moisture lover and a strong, fast grower. Needs semi-shade in summer.

- WHEN TO PRUNE Pinch only when repotting, then again in fall.
- WHEN TO REPOT Early spring/early summer.
- WHEN TO FERTILIZE Late winter/early spring.
- WHEN TO WATER Needs frequent watering as needed.

SUITABLE VARIETIES

babylonica (Weeping) Hardy to zone 5.
purpurea 'Nana' (Dwarf purple osier) Hardy to zone 5.

SEQUOIA (REDWOOD)

- STYLES Formal upright, informal upright, slanting, twin trunk, driftwood, clump, forest.
- TEMPERATURE Needs indoor climate during winter.
- INDOOR/OUTDOOR
- HARDINESS RATING Hardy to zone 7.
- NON-FLOWERING
- EVERGREEN

The famed California redwood. A giant in nature and a most interesting bonsai. Has interesting red-brown bark, and needle-like leaves. Tolerates light shade but prefers sun.

- WHEN TO PRUNE Early spring.
- WHEN TO REPOT Early spring.
- WHEN TO FERTILIZE Early spring and fall.
- WHEN TO WATER Frequently.

SUITABLE VARIETY

sempervirens (Coast redwood) Hardy to zone 7.

SERISSA (SNOW ROSE)

- STYLES Informal upright, slanting, cascade, semicascade, literati, exposed root, root-over-rock, clinging-to-rock, twin trunk, clump, raft, sinuous, saikei.
- TEMPERATURE Greenhouse or house temperatures during fall, winter and spring, with slightly cooler nights than days.
- INDOOR
- HARDINESS RATING Hardy to zone 9.
- FLOWERING
- EVERGREEN

An indoor plant. Flowers are small and white. Needs as much light as possible. Available in most houseplant nurseries.

- WHEN TO PRUNE When in growth and when the new shoots have developed

Details of the flowers and leaves of Serissa foetida *Snow rose.*

several nodes, prune to within one to two nodes of trunk.
- WHEN TO REPOT Spring.
- WHEN TO FERTILIZE Once a month during the growing season.
- WHEN TO WATER Frequently.

SUITABLE VARIETIES

crassiramea (Makino) A broad-leafed shrub that bears white flowers. Prefers full sun.
foetida Excellent bonsai material with leaves and flowers in scale with the desired look. White flowers can be single or double. Emits a faint fetid odor when cut. 'Variegata' has green leaves with yellow margins.

STEWARTIA

- STYLES Informal upright, slanting, root-over-rock, twin trunk, clump.
- TEMPERATURE Differs according to variety.
- OUTDOOR
- HARDINESS RATING Moderately hardy to zone 7.
- FLOWERING
- DECIDUOUS

A lime-hating shrub or small tree, with oval leaves and good fall color.

- WHEN TO PRUNE When flowers have shriveled, but before the new buds have hardened.
- WHEN TO REPOT Early spring.
- WHEN TO FERTILIZE Early spring, fall.
- WHEN TO WATER Frequently.

SUITABLE VARIETIES

monadelpha Hardy to zone 8.
pseudocamellia (Japanese) White flowers, hardy to zone 8.

TAMARIX (TAMARISK)

- STYLES Informal upright, slanting, cascade, semicascade, root-over-rock, clinging-to-rock, twin trunk, clump, two and three tree grouping, saikei.
- TEMPERATURE Differs slightly according to variety.
- OUTDOOR
- HARDINESS RATING Hardy to zones 3–7, depending on variety.
- FLOWERING
- DECIDUOUS

A hardy shrub with beautiful scale-like leaves and small-scale flowers. Even if you live beside the sea, this plant will do well since it tolerates salt spray. Most are native to desert-like areas. Easily found in local and specialist nurseries.

- WHEN TO PRUNE Allow long new shoots to develop, then prune drastically in fall.
- WHEN TO REPOT Spring.
- WHEN TO FERTILIZE Early spring, early summer, fall.
- WHEN TO WATER Keep plant wet at all times.

SUITABLE VARIETIES

chinensis (Juniper). The least hardy variety, this has purplish-pink flowers in spring and summer.
parviflora (Small-flower) Pink and hardy.
ramoisissima (Odessa)

Details of the trunks and leaves of Stewartia monadelpha *Stewartia.*

TAXODIUM (BALD CYPRESS)

- STYLES Formal upright, informal upright, slanted, split trunk, driftwood, clinging-to-rock, twin trunk, clump, forest.
- TEMPERATURE Differs slightly according to variety.
- OUTDOOR
- HARDINESS RATING Hardy to zone 5, depending on variety.
- NON-FLOWERING
- EVERGREEN

A most interesting subject for bonsai. Inhabits wet areas such as swamps and has "knees" growing upward from the roots, projecting above the water. You are more likely to find specimens in a bonsai or a mail-order nursery.

- WHEN TO PRUNE Pinch tips of new buds during their growth spurts throughout the year.
- WHEN TO REPOT Late spring.
- WHEN TO FERTILIZE Early spring, early summer, fall.
- WHEN TO WATER Keep consistently damp.

SUITABLE VARIETY

distichum (Bald cypress, Swamp cypress) Hardy to zone 5.

TAXUS (YEW)

- STYLES Formal upright, informal upright, split trunk, twin trunk, clump.
- TEMPERATURE Differs according to variety.
- OUTDOOR
- HARDINESS RATING Hardy to zones 5–7, depending on variety.
- NON-FLOWERING
- EVERGREEN

An evergreen conifer whose ease in growing and hardiness have made it popular for bonsai. Its foliage is dark green and its growth pattern lends itself to formal styling. The female tree bears fruits with red arils, which gives it added value as bonsai material. Prefers semi-shade. Found in nurseries, with rarer varieties at bonsai nurseries in seedling and seed forms.

- WHEN TO PRUNE Pinch the ends of the new buds whenever you want to during the growing season. However, if a display of fruit is desired, postpone any pruning until after the "flowers" appear, taking care to leave the spent flower nodes on the bonsai and just trim the new growth.
- WHEN TO REPOT Spring to fall.
- WHEN TO FERTILIZE Spring and fall.
- WHEN TO WATER Regularly.

SUITABLE VARIETIES

baccata (English) Hardy to zone 7 but some cultivars are hardier.
brevifolia (Western) Hardy to zone 6.
chinensis (Chinese) Hardy to zone 6.
cuspidata (Japanese) Hardy to zone 5. Suitable varieties include *T.c.* 'Nana' (dwarf).
media A hybrid, hardy to zone 5.

TRACHELOSPERMUM (CONFEDERATE JASMINE)

- STYLES Informal upright, slanting, cascade, semicascade, literati, root-over-rock, clinging-to-rock, twin trunk, clump, saikei.

- TEMPERATURE 45–65°F.
- OUTDOOR/INDOOR
- HARDINESS RATING Hardy to zone 8, depending on variety.
- FLOWERING
- EVERGREEN In warmer climates.

Hardy in warmer climates, indoor or greenhouse plants in colder climates. Known for their fragrance. Available in indoor nurseries.

- WHEN TO PRUNE Following flowering, trim shoots that have several buds back to the one or two nodes closest to the trunk.
- WHEN TO REPOT Late spring to fall.
- WHEN TO FERTILIZE Early spring, summer, and fall. Responds well to manure tea.
- WHEN TO WATER Frequently.

SUITABLE VARIETY

asiaticum (Yellow star) Yellow. Hardy to zone 8.

TSUGA (HEMLOCK)

- STYLES Formal upright, informal upright, slanting, twin trunk, clump, raft, sinuous, forest, saikei.
- TEMPERATURE Differs according to variety.
- OUTDOOR
- HARDINESS RATING Hardy to zones 3–7, depending on variety.
- NON-FLOWERING
- EVERGREEN

A hardy conifer, readily found in local nurseries. During the summer, it prefers semi-shade. More exotic varieties are found in bonsai nurseries in seedling and seed forms.

- WHEN TO PRUNE Pinch several times in

Detail of the foliage of Taxus cuspidata *Japanese yew.*

spring; pinch tips off before new growth hardens, leaving a small cluster of needles at the base.
- WHEN TO REPOT Repot in spring before new shoots expand.
- WHEN TO FERTILIZE Late winter/early spring.
- WHEN TO WATER Frequently, as long as it drains thoroughly afterwards.

SUITABLE VARIETIES

canadensis (Canadian, Common) Hardy to zone 3.
diversifolia (Japanese) Hardy to zone 6.
heterophylla (Western) Hardy to zone 7.
sieboldii (Japanese) Hardy to zone 6.

ULMUS (ELM)

- STYLES Informal upright, slanting, broom, twin trunk, clump, forest.
- TEMPERATURE Differs very slightly according to variety.
- OUTDOOR/INDOOR
- HARDINESS RATING Hardy to zones 3–7, depending on variety.
- FLOWERS INSIGNIFICANT
- EVERGREEN/DECIDUOUS

Hardy in warmer climates, with fine ramification of branches possible.

- WHEN TO PRUNE Following the growth

period, when there are several nodes on new growth, prune leaving the one or two nodes closest to the main branch or trunk.
- WHEN TO REPOT Early spring.
- WHEN TO FERTILIZE Late winter/early spring.
- WHEN TO WATER Moderately.

SUITABLE VARIETIES

carpinifolia (Smooth-leafed)
davidiana japonica Hardy to zone 6.
parvifolia (Chinese) Hardy to zone 6.
procera (English) Hardy to zone 6.

VIBURNUM

- STYLES Informal upright, slanting, cascade, semicascade, root-over-rock, twin trunk, clump.
- TEMPERATURE Differs according to variety.
- OUTDOOR
- HARDINESS RATING Most evergreen varieties hardy to zone 5, most deciduous varieties hardy to zone 3.
- FLOWERING
- DECIDUOUS/EVERGREEN

Green leaves of varying sizes and shapes, depending on variety, most turning red to mahogany in fall. Flowers are white and off-white, appearing in late spring, with berries that follow in the fall. Most viburnums are relatively pest-free. Found at speciality nurseries. Requires full sun.

- WHEN TO PRUNE After blooming when flowers have shriveled but before new buds harden.
- WHEN TO REPOT Early spring.
- WHEN TO FERTILIZE Early spring, fall.
- WHEN TO WATER Frequently.

SUITABLE VARIETIES

dilatatum Deciduous; with large leaves; hardy to zone 5.
opulus 'Nanum' (European dwarf cranberry bush, Guelder rose, Whitten tree) Deciduous; hardy to zone 3.

plicatum tomentosum 'Mariesii' (Double-file) Deciduous; hardy to zone 5.
prunifolium (Black haw, Sweet haw, Sheepberry, Nannyberry, Stagbush) Hardy to zone 3.

WEIGELA

- STYLES Informal upright, slanting, cascade, semicascade, twin trunk, clump.
- TEMPERATURE Differs according to variety.
- OUTDOOR
- HARDINESS RATING Hardy to zone 5.
- FLOWERING
- DECIDUOUS

Excellent broad-leafed plants not commonly used, but found in old gardens and nurseries. Blooms in late spring on last year's growth. Place in semi-shade.

- WHEN TO PRUNE Since flowering occurs on year-old wood, prune after flowering. Do not prune the following spring or you will eliminate flowering for the season.
- WHEN TO REPOT Early spring.
- WHEN TO FERTILIZE Early spring, early summer, fall.
- WHEN TO WATER Keep evenly moist. Plant does not like to dry out.

SUITABLE VARIETIES

florida Rose flowers. Hardy to zone 5. Cultivars include 'Bristol Ruby,' 'Eva Rathke' have dark-red flowers and the smallest leaves.
praecox (Early rose) The earliest to flower with rose blossoms. Hardy to zone 5.

WISTERIA

- STYLES Informal upright, slanting, cascade, semicascade, coiled.
- TEMPERATURE 20–60°F according to variety.
- OUTDOOR
- HARDINESS RATING Hardy to zones 5–9,

Detail of the flowers of Wisteria floribunda *Japanese wisteria.*

depending on variety.
- FLOWERING Lavender to white flowers in pendulous racemes.
- DECIDUOUS

Hardy, winding, and woody plant which makes spectacular bonsai. Old plants found in old gardens, new plants in nurseries. Old specimens develop gnarled trunks and prominent roots. After flowering the plant develops seed pods; remove most or all. Expose to full sun except in the hottest part of the summer.

- WHEN TO PRUNE In summer, after blooming, pinch out most young shoots, leaving only two to three buds. Before leaves harden, eliminate or reduce side branches. After the leaves fall, prune side branches. If heavy pruning is necessary, do it in winter. Flowers develop on the branches that are the shortest trailers, so you have a choice of keeping the longest trailers for effect, if you like. Due to the nature of this strong vine, pruning is frequently appropriate but remember that blooming occurs on old wood. Needs protection from frost.
- WHEN TO REPOT Every year in early spring, in a container deep enough to retain some moisture. If planted in shallow container for effect, watch the plant's water requirements carefully.

Alternatively, repot in fall. Be careful of easily broken, fleshy roots, trimming only the smaller roots if possible. Never cut the long tap root.
- WHEN TO FERTILIZE Beginning in early spring, feed once a month until flowers have finished, then stop feeding. Feed again in late summer. If tree is freshly repotted, wait at least two months before feeding. Manure and manure tea feedings are useful in encouraging prolific flowering.
- WHEN TO WATER Water copiously to keep evenly moist but avoid plant sitting in water constantly unless the temperature is extremely high. Fine roots will rot if too wet and will dry out or burn if too dry. Air circulation must be good.

SUITABLE VARIETIES

floribunda (Japanese) Violet to violet-blue, white, red, or pink. Fragrant. Hardy to zone 5.
macrostachya (Kentucky) Flowers are blue, lilac, or purple. Hardy to zone 6.
sinensis (Chinese, Sweet) Violet blue and not fragrant. Hardy to zone 5.
venusta (Silky) White and fragrant and the earliest to flower. Hardy to zone 5.

ZELKOVA (JAPANESE "ELM")

- STYLE Broom, a singular style ideally suited to the natural growth habit of the genus. The name comes from the old-fashioned brooms, where twigs tied together were then attached to a larger branch which served as the handle.
- TEMPERATURE Protect from frost, exact temperatures differ according to variety.
- OUTDOOR Needs winter protection.
- HARDINESS RATING Hardy to zone 5.
- FLOWERS INCONSPICUOUS
- DECIDUOUS

Hardy and a popular choice for bonsai. Easy-to-grow trees with distinctive branch configuration, interesting bark, and yellow/red color in fall. This is an elegant and formal tree, perfect when styled with one or more trees, single trunk, straight form in an earthenware container. Available in some nurseries and from bonsai specialists in seedling or seed form.

- WHEN TO PRUNE *Zelkova* is a fast grower. It requires constant attention to its pruning requirements. Prune shoots from spring to fall, leaving only a couple of leaves on each branch so good branch structure is achieved. Prune some buds off. Leaf prune in early summer, but only those trees which are healthy. Major pruning in winter.

- WHEN TO REPOT Every year in early spring. Prune half the roots at the same time and pot into a container one size larger, if necessary.

- WHEN TO FERTILIZE If tree has just been repotted, wait six to eight weeks before feeding. In off years, feed in spring and fall. Organic fertilizer is preferable. Do not feed in mid/late summer; do not feed an unhealthy tree.

- WHEN TO WATER Water sparingly in winter, increase slightly in spring and fall, drench in summer. Allow soil to dry out between waterings. Mist foliage in summer.

SUITABLE VARIETY

serrata (Saw-leaf) Sharply toothed oval leaves, hence its common name.

Everything in Omiya is in sympathy with the town's main industry – bonsai. Even the signposts, such as this one for a bonsai nursery, are in wood.

Index

143

Author's acknowledgments

Bonsai and its study has had a great impact on my life. Gardening in Woodmere and Hewlett Harbor, Long Island, New York until 1978, bonsai kept me from doing such mundane things as laundry, while it allowed me to acquire a wide scope of plant material for a veritable botanical garden in a very small space.

It taught me about pruning and potting for health and beauty; appreciation of fine horticultural detail; characteristics of plants; seasonal changes and how to cope with them. But, most important, bonsai taught me patience.

The person who unknowingly brought me to the garden's edge and bade me jump in was my father, Marshall Francis Bachenheimer, a remarkable man, as comfortable on the golf course or behind a microphone for an advertising campaign as he was in the garden. I know I inherited his commitment to beauty and growing things. Thanks Dad.

The man to whom I truly owe my love of, appreciation for, and sense of adventure in, bonsai, is Dr Albert Fine, now of Longmeadow, Massachusetts. He and his wife, Shirley, all of us passionate gardeners, became my neighbors and dear friends in Woodmere. In his garden, Al had a bonsai collection. As a collector of many things, and an artist of sorts, I was quickly drawn to bonsai. Seeing this, Al took me under his tutorial wing. I continued my education with such consummate professionals as Frank Okamura at the Brooklyn Botanic Garden, Yuji Yoshimura at the New York Botanical Garden, and John Naka, among others.

Gradually, bonsai people found each other, and soon Al, Martin Haber, of Hewlett, Long Island, and I co-founded the South Shore Bonsai Workshop, inspired by membership in the Long Island Bonsai Society, New York Bonsai Society, American Bonsai Society, and Bonsai Clubs International. I thank them all.

Professionally, I must thank Karen Jeffers of Levett, Rockwood and Sanders, attorneys in Westport, Connecticut. And I send unending hugs to my sons John and James, my mother, Rae Bachenheimer, herself a writer and gardener, and my friends Marjorie St Aubyn, Sherry Becker, and Judy Cunningham, all of whom were cheerleaders whenever one was needed. Last, I must give my special thanks to beautiful, verdant Easton, Connecticut, my home, which through it all wrapped me in nature's beauty and kept me sane.

Publisher's acknowledgments

Swallow Publishing would like to thank the Brooklyn Botanic Garden for giving access for photography to their bonsai collection; John Ainsworth, of Tokonoma Bonsai, Radlett, Herts, for his help with the step-by-step photography; Elizabeth Scholtz for supplying caption information; and Edmund Moulin, Dr Stephen K-M. Tim and Barbara Pesch of BBG for their invaluable work on this edition.

Photographic credits

p11 The Bridgeman Art Library; p12 Mary Evans Picture Library; p13 The Bridgeman Art Library; p43 Dr DW Larson, University of Guelph.